# Clue

BASED ON THE SCREENPLAY BY
**JONATHAN LYNN**

WRITTEN BY
**SANDY RUSTIN**
ADDITIONAL MATERIAL BY
**HUNTER FOSTER AND ERIC PRICE**

BASED ON THE PARAMOUNT PICTURES MOTION PICTURE
BASED ON THE HASBRO BOARD GAME CLUE

## DPS

DRAMATISTS PLAY SERVICE

# Cast of Characters

**WADSWORTH**, a traditional British butler in every sense: uptight, formal, and "by the book." He is the driving force in the play.

**YVETTE**, a loyal and sexy French maid.

**MISS SCARLET**, a dry, sardonic D.C. madam, more interested in secrets than sex.

**MRS. PEACOCK**, the wealthy wife of a senator. A bit batty, neurotic, and quick to hysteria.

**MRS. WHITE**, a pale, morbid, and tragic woman. Mrs. White may or may not be the murderer of her five ex-husbands.

**COLONEL MUSTARD**, a puffy, pompous, dense, blowhard of a military man.

**PROFESSOR PLUM**, an arrogant academic, easily impressed by himself.

**MR. GREEN**, a timid, yet officious, rule follower. He's awfully anxious.

**ENSEMBLE WOMAN**

> **THE COOK**, a gruff woman with a threatening presence. (Alive and Dead.)

> **SINGING TELEGRAM GIRL**, a tap dancer with a heart of gold. (Alive and Dead.)

> **AUXILIARY SCARLET**, the back of Miss Scarlet during a scene of theatrical trickery. (Can also be played by an offstage cover.)

> **BACKUP COP**, backup for the Chief in the very final "Cops" entrance.

**ENSEMBLE MAN 1**

> **MR. BODDY**, a slick, Frank Sinatra, film noir-esque type fella. (Alive and Dead.)

> **THE MOTORIST**, a professional driver. (Alive and Dead.)

> **CHIEF OF POLICE**, a cop who helps to save the day.

**ENSEMBLE MAN 2**

> **THE UNEXPECTED COP,** a regular joe. (Alive and Dead.)
> **BACKUP COP,** a backup for the Chief.
> **AUXILIARY MUSTARD,** the back of Colonel Mustard during a scene of theatrical trickery. (Can also be played by an offstage cover.)

PLEASE NOTE: An additional body to play the DEAD MOTORIST in the Lounge during Scene 11 is required. Perhaps an understudy or ASM can fill in for this sixty-second moment of comedic razzle-dazzle.

## TIME

The play begins just before dinner on a dark and stormy night not too far from Washington, D.C., in 1954.

## PLACE

Boddy Manor. A mansion of epic proportions and terrifying secrets.

## SET

The interior of Boddy Manor. A grand hallway of á large, imposing, Gothic Victorian house (gloomy and menacing) is the focal point of the play. Doors that lead to the Library, the Study, the Lounge, the Billiard Room, the Conservatory, the Ballroom, the Kitchen, and the Dining Room line the Hall. The set is such that the various rooms of Boddy Manor easily pull out/appear in surprising ways, making transitions from one area of the house to another very fast.

# PRODUCTION NOTES

*Clue* is a highly stylized ensemble piece. It is to be played with honesty and truth. The "life or death" stakes of the situation are more important than comic bits. The pacing of *Clue* is intended to be very swift. This script maps out suggested physicality in some cases, but casts are encouraged to embrace the style and find their own moments of comedic physicality while maintaining a truthful intention throughout.

The play is intended to be scored.

It is worth noting for context that this play takes place at the height of McCarthyism and the Red Scare. By definition, McCarthyism is the practice of making accusations of subversion or treason without proper regard for evidence. How apropos. No?

# CLUE

## Prologue

*A scrim hangs at the front of the stage reproducing the exterior of Boddy Manor. Thunder. Lightning illuminates the theatre. The scrim rises.*

*Ominous, urgent music plays. Sounds of heavy rain. Dimly lit wall sconces and chandeliers reveal an empty regal foyer and magnificent front Hall.*

*Yvette (a sexy French maid, dressed perfectly) polishes a glass while watching the news on a static-filled black-and-white television set.*

**NEWSCASTER'S VOICE.** McCarthy's shrieking denunciations and fearmongering have created a climate of fear and suspicion across the country—raising the question in households across the nation: Who are the un-American Americans amongst us?

*A startling crash of thunder/lightning illuminates the glass-paneled front door, revealing the silhouette of a man holding an umbrella.*

*Senator McCarthy's voice is heard from the TV.*

**MCCARTHY'S VOICE.** "Any man who has been named by either a senator of a committee or a congressman is dangerous to the welfare of this nation."

*The front door creaks open, unheard by Yvette.*

*Enter Wadsworth, the butler, dressed perfectly, shaking off and stowing his umbrella and hat, a twinkle in his eye.*

**NEWSCASTER'S VOICE.** President Eisenhower refuses to engage directly with McCarthy. In a letter to his brother however, Eisenhower explains— "as for McCarthy—only a shortsighted or completely inexperienced individual would urge the use of the office of the presidency to give an opponent the publicity he so avidly desires.

*Wadsworth moves behind Yvette.*

*(Beneath the following dialogue until cut off.)* "Time and time again, without apology or evasion, I—and many members of this administration—have stood for the right of the individual, for free expression of convictions, even though those convictions might be unpopular, and for uncensored use of our libraries, except as dictated by common decency."

**WADSWORTH.** *(Rather intimately.)* Yvette?

*Yvette yelps, startled!*

**YVETTE.** Monsieur! I didn't hear you come in! You frightened me half to death!

**WADSWORTH.** Wouldn't want to do that. There are so many better ways to die. *(Then.)* Please turn off that noise.

*Yvette turns off the TV—cutting off the news.*

Is everything ready?

**YVETTE.** Oui.

**WADSWORTH.** Good. *(Calling off.)* Cook?

*In a flash of thunder/lightning, a formidable Cook, dressed perfectly, appears from the Kitchen.*

**COOK.** You called, sir?

**WADSWORTH.** Everything on schedule?

**COOK.** Dinner will be ready at 7:30. *(Revealing a butcher knife on a music sting.)* Sharp.

*Just then, the doorbell rings. They look out.*

**WADSWORTH.** Ah. Right on time. You have your instructions?

**YVETTE.** Oui.

**WADSWORTH.** Very well then.

*He moves to the door. Yvette pushes off the TV. The Cook exits to the Kitchen.*

*(Just before opening the door.)* Let the game begin.

<h1 align="center">Scene 1</h1>



*The Hall/The Lounge.*

*Wadsworth grandly opens the front door to a music sting.*

*Colonel Mustard, officious, stands in the doorway, shielding himself from the rain. He wears a decorated Colonel's uniform.*

*The Cook reenters during the following to assist with coats and such.*

**WADSWORTH.**  Good evening.

**MUSTARD.**  *(Entering fully.)* Good evening. I'm not sure if I'm in the right—

**WADSWORTH.**  Yes, indeed you are expected, Colonel.

**MUSTARD.**  How do you— *(Know who I am?)*

**WADSWORTH.**  *(Interrupting.)* It is Colonel Mustard, isn't it?

**MUSTARD.**  No, that's not my name. My name is Colonel—

**WADSWORTH.**  *(Interrupting again.)* I believe it's been recommended that tonight you use a pseudonym.

**MUSTARD.**  Oh, no thank you. I took an antihistamine before I came.

**WADSWORTH.**  *(Taking his coat.)* May I take your coat?

**MUSTARD.**  Oh. All right. I suppose I…

> *Yvette, at the bar cart, now pops open a bottle of champagne, á la a gunshot, startling Mustard, who yelps—interrupting himself.*

**WADSWORTH.**  Not to worry, Colonel. It's just the maid, in the Hall, with the champagne cork.

**YVETTE.**  *(Offering.)* Champagne?

**MUSTARD.**  *(Taking the glass, flummoxed by her beauty.)* Oh, uh, don't mind if I…

**YVETTE.**  *(Interrupting.)* Zis way monsieur.

**MUSTARD.**  *(Following her anywhere.)* Ah. Thank you.

> *Yvette escorts Mustard to the door of the Lounge. The doorbell interrupts. They look out.*

Are you expecting someone else?

**WADSWORTH.**  Indeed. I'll be with you in a moment.

**YVETTE.**  Follow me, Colonel.

**MUSTARD.**  With pleasure, my dear.

> *Yvette opens the Lounge door, escorting Mustard inside.*
>
> *Wadsworth opens the front door to a music sting.*
>
> *Mrs. White stands, tragic and morbid, dressed in funeral clothing, guarding herself from the rain. Over her face is a mesh black veil.*

**WADSWORTH.**  Do come in, madam. You are expected.

> *She enters more fully, Wadsworth at her heels.*

Welcome.

**WHITE.**  *(With a confident mystique.)* Do you know who I am?

> *She pulls back her veil to reveal her face.*

**WADSWORTH.**  Only that you are a socialite to be known this evening as Mrs. White.

> *She slips off her cloak, black with a brilliantly white inside.*

**WHITE.**  Yes.

> *Wadsworth catches it gracefully.*

It said so in my letter. But, why—?

**WADSWORTH.**  *(Interrupting.)* May I introduce you? Mrs. White, this is the maid, Yvette.

> *Music sting as the women notice each other and flinch.*

I see you two know each other.

**WHITE.**  *(Deliberately lying.)* We've never met.

**YVETTE.**  *(Cheekily.)* Champagne?

**WHITE.**  *(Pointedly.)* I think not.

**WADSWORTH.**  Please, warm yourself in the Lounge.

**WHITE.**  Why? Do I look cold?

**WADSWORTH.** A bit. *(Shepherding her into the Lounge—then.)* I'll be right with you. This way please.

> *The module of the set containing the door to the Lounge now pulls open slightly, making the interior of the Lounge partially visible as White steps through the door, noticing Mustard.*

**WHITE.** Oh. Hello.

**MUSTARD.** Hello. Pleased to meet you.

**WHITE.** I'm rarely pleased to meet anyone.

> *Doorbell rings. They look out.*

More?

**WADSWORTH.** Oh, yes.

> *Wadsworth shuts the Lounge door, closing the module back up. Yvette opens the front door to a music sting. Mrs. Peacock, middle-aged, wealthy, batty, and impressed with herself, stands covered in jewels, a foxtail-fur stole, and a hat of peacock feathers, shielding herself from the rain with a box of candy.*

**YVETTE.** Bonjour madame. Pleaze, come in from ze rain.

> *As Peacock enters…*

**WADSWORTH.** Mrs. Peacock, I presume.

**PEACOCK.** Who?! *(Realizing.)* Oh yes! That's me!

**WADSWORTH.** Cook, will you please take Mrs. Peacock's stole.

> *With a music sting, the women recognize each other. They flinch!*

I see you two know each other.

**PEACOCK.** *(Discarding her stole into the Cook's arms.)* Don't be ridiculous, I've never seen this woman before in my life.

**YVETTE.** *(Offering.)* Champagne?

**PEACOCK.** My lips belong to the Lord!

**WADSWORTH.** Please, make yourself comfortable in the Lounge.

**PEACOCK.** Thank you.

> *As Wadsworth escorts her to the Lounge, she remembers the lavishly wrapped box of chocolates in her hands.*

Oh! For your hospitality… *(An aside.)* And there's a coupla Benjamins hidden under the caramels for you, Butler.

**WADSWORTH.**  How…sticky.

**PEACOCK.**  I expect to be treated like the wife of a…

*The doorbell rings, interrupting her. They look out.*

**WADSWORTH.**  Hold that thought. This way please. After you, Mrs. Peacock.

*He opens the door (module) to the Lounge; the interior becomes halfway visible.*

**PEACOCK.**  *(Enamored by the doorframe.)* Oh my, look at the detail of this molding; this is quite a magnificent mansion, isn't it…

*She screams, startled to find White and Mustard.*

Who are you?!

**WHITE.**  Welcome to the party.

**MUSTARD.**  *(Tickled pink.)* This is turning out to be quite the crowd.

*Yvette closes the Lounge door (module retreats). Wadsworth opens the front door to a music sting, Rottweiler dogs bark. Mr. Green, straight as an arrow, stands in a trench coat, holding an umbrella. He does not enter, but remains in the doorway, anxious.*

**GREEN.**  Is this the right address to meet a…Mr. Boddy?

*The dogs bark wildly.*

**WADSWORTH.**  *(To dogs.)* Sit!

*Green frantically sits. Dogs stop barking.*

No. Not you, sir.

*Green stands sheepishly.*

**GREEN.**  Sorry, sorry.

**WADSWORTH.**  Please, come in.

**GREEN.**  *(Entering more fully.)* Excuse me, I suppose this letter has me rather anxious.

**WADSWORTH.**  You must be Mr. Green.

**GREEN.**  *(Painfully lying.)* Yes. That's exactly who I am.

**WADSWORTH.**  Welcome, sir.

*Green hands his umbrella to Yvette as he steps into the Hall.*

**GREEN.**  *(Noticing the interior.)* Whoa. This isn't at all what I expected.

**WADSWORTH.**  I find if you expect nothing, you're never disappointed.

**GREEN.**  *(Not to be misunderstood.)* Oh, I'm not disappointed…

> *The doorbell rings, interrupting.*

> *They look out.*

**WADSWORTH.**  Pardon me, sir.

> *Wadsworth moves up to the door.*

**GREEN.**  *(Overwhelmed by the expansive mansion—to himself.)* Holy cow…

> *Wadsworth opens the door (music sting) to find Professor Plum (smoking a pipe) with Miss Scarlet (smoking a long, thin cigarette) standing behind him.*

**WADSWORTH.**  Good evening.

**PLUM.**  *(Reading authoritatively from his letter in the doorway.)* "Please arrive at 7:30 sharp on Saturday evening." *(A glance to his watch.)* Well, here I am…

**WADSWORTH.**  Professor Plum.

**PLUM.**  If you say so.

**SCARLET.**  *(Stepping in more fully.)* Well, well, well. And I thought I'd seen everything…

**WADSWORTH.**  Miss Scarlet. Welcome. I didn't realize you and the Professor were acquainted.

**SCARLET.**  We're not.

> *Scarlet continues as Plum gives his coat to Cook. He wears an academic suit. If he weren't so off-putting, he'd be charming.*

The bridge is washed out from the rain. My car broke down, and this Professor offered to give me a ride.

**PLUM.**  *(Smarmily to Green.)* I'm hoping she'll return the favor one day.

**SCARLET.**  Subtle. *(Back to Wadsworth.)* I didn't realize we were headed to the same place until…we arrived.

> *Dialogue continues as Scarlet gives her coat to the Cook. She looks positively Hollywood in a provocative dress. If she*

*weren't such a broad, she'd be classy. Green also hands his coat to the Cook.*

**WADSWORTH.** *(To Plum.)* How was your drive?

**PLUM.** It's a long haul.

**WADSWORTH.** Indeed, it is a long hall. But then, it's a very large house. *(Then.)* This way please.

*Wadsworth points the way to the Lounge. Scarlet absorbs the grandeur of the manor.*

**SCARLET.** Say…what is this godforsaken place anyway?

**WADSWORTH.** This old place? Oh, this…is Boddy Manor.

*Thunder/lightning. They jump. Green more so than the others.* Cook. Dinner?

**COOK.** Directly.

*The Cook moves to exit.*

**WADSWORTH.** *(Showing Scarlet, Plum, and Green to the Lounge.)* Appetizers in the Lounge. After you.

*The Lounge module now opens fully to reveal the interior.*

**PLUM.** Hors d'oeuvres. Good. I'm starving.

**GREEN.** Funny. I haven't much of an appetite at all.

**SCARLET.** *(Entering the Lounge and noticing the others.)* My, my, this really is a party.

**PLUM.** *(As he enters the Lounge.)* Well, greetings all. It's a pleasure for you to see me. *(Noticing drinks, he helps himself.)* Oooh, cocktail hour!

**GREEN.** *(As he enters the Lounge.)* There are so many of you—I didn't realize…

**WADSWORTH.** *(Interrupting.)* Right. Good then. You're all here. *(Then, swiftly paced.)* Colonel Mustard.

**MUSTARD.** Present.

**WADSWORTH.** Miss Scarlet.

**SCARLET.** Hmm.

**WADSWORTH.** Mrs. White.

**WHITE.** Yes.

**WADSWORTH.** Professor Plum.

**PLUM.** Right.

**WADSWORTH.** Mr. Green.

**GREEN.** That's me.

**WADSWORTH.** Mrs. Peacock.

**PEACOCK.** *(With a rather formal, yet floppy, curtsey.)* How d'you do?

**WADSWORTH.** Greetings. I am Wadsworth, the butler. *(Then.)* Tonight, as you may have surmised, nobody is being addressed by their real name. A courtesy your host has provided to ensure your privacy. I suggest you follow his lead and refrain from revealing too much about yourselves this evening. For you never know when—

> *The Cook strikes a gong, interrupting. They jump! Green spills champagne all over himself.*

*(Calmly, as always.)* Ah. Dinner.

**GREEN.** *(Wiping himself up.)* Oh, sorry. Sorry. I'm a bit clumsy, I suppose.

**PLUM.** Dinner? That was more like a cocktail minute.

**SCARLET.** Mr. Wadsworth, you were saying…"You never know when"…what?

**WADSWORTH.** What?

**SCARLET.** What?

**WADSWORTH.** Hm? *(Then—showing the way.)* This way please.

> *Yvette has handed Green a fresh glass of champagne just in time for the Cook (who has reentered) to hit the gong again. They jump! Green spills his drink again.*

We really oughtn't keep her waiting. Cook can get cranky. Ladies and gentlemen, follow me. The Dining Room is right this way.

> *Transition music. The cast follows Wadsworth from the Lounge to the Dining Room. Behind them as the Lounge module closes, the Dining Room wall flies in, and Yvette and the Cook each push on one side of a Dining Room table (with chairs) that meets in the middle.*

## Scene 2

*The Dining Room.*

*The guests arrive to find a beautifully set table with seven places.*

**WADSWORTH.** You'll find your names beside your places. Please be seated.

> *Suspicious of each other, the guests are hesitant to take their seats.*

**ALL.** *(Ad-libbing.)* There are assigned seats? / I prefer to sit by the door. / Do you see my tag? / Is that me? / Is that you? / Oh, here you are, Mr. Green. *(Etc.)*

> *They take their places, Mustard next to Scarlet next to Green next to Peacock next to White next to Plum.*

**MUSTARD.** *(Not yet seated.)* This place—at the head of the table—is that for you?

**WADSWORTH.** Indeed no, sir. I don't sit. I am merely a humble butler.

**MUSTARD.** What exactly do you do?

**WADSWORTH.** I buttle, sir.

**COOK.** *(Presenting the meal grandly.)* Dinner is served.

**WADSWORTH.** Thank you, Cook.

> *As the guests settle in their seats, Yvette and the Cook serve them soup (off of trays). The guests look at each other with a mixture of interest and suspicion, each an individual Sherlock Holmes throughout.*
>
> *Peacock taps her knife against her glass to get the guests' attention. (The waving of her knife is a bit threatening to Green beside her.)*

**PEACOCK.** *(Tucking a napkin in at her neck á la a bib.)* All right then, what's all this about, Butler, this dinner party? And where is our host?

**WADSWORTH.** "Ours not to reason why,
Ours but to do and die..."

**GREEN.** *(Anxiously.)* Die?

  *Thunder clap. The guests startle.*

**WADSWORTH.** Merely quoting, sir, from Alfred, Lord Tennyson.

**SCARLET.** I prefer Kipling myself. *(Offering a basket of dinner rolls to Mustard.)* Do you like Kipling, Colonel?

**MUSTARD.** *(Helping himself.)* Sure, I'll eat anything. *(Then.)* So, if this seat is not for you, Butler, then who's it for? Is there a seventh guest?

**GREEN.** Seven is my lucky number.

**WHITE.** A seventh guest? I thought you said we were all here?

**PEACOCK.** How many people are coming to this party anyway?!

**WADSWORTH.** *(Pouring wine.)* All in good time, friends.

**PLUM.** Well, what kind of host serves dinner before everyone's arrived?

  *As Yvette serves soup to Scarlet.*

**YVETTE.** Not to worry, monsieur; I will keep something warm for him.

**SCARLET.** *(Acidly.)* What did you have in mind, dear?

  *As Yvette serves soup to Peacock—*

**PEACOCK.** What is that smell? It's something…familiar.

**YVETTE.** Shark's fin soup.

**PEACOCK.** *(Gleefully.)* My favorite!

**COOK.** *(Deliberately.)* I know.

  *With a music sting, the Cook and Peacock exchange a sinister glance.*

**YVETTE.** Bon appétit!

  *Yvette and the Cook exit. The guests—tension in the air—sip their soup.*

**PEACOCK.** *(Immediately eating voraciously.)* Oh my, this soup is delicious, isn't it? *(Loving it.)* Yum, yum, yum, yummy yummy, yum, yum. (Then, perhaps with a choke, now noticing all eyes on her,* *nearly in one breath—as Wadsworth pours wine.)* Well, somebody's got to break the ice, might as well be me. I mean, I'm used to being a hostess, it's part of my husband's work, so I'm perfectly prepared to get the ball rolling, I mean, I have absolutely no idea what we're all doing here but I'm determined to enjoy myself and I'm very intrigued and oh, my, this soup is *delicious* isn't it?

> *The guests stare at her, bewildered.*

**WHITE.**  You say you're used to being a hostess, Mrs. Peacock?

**PEACOCK.**  Yes. It's an integral part of my life as the wife of a… *(Stopping herself.)* Oh dear, I forgot, we're not supposed to say who we *really* are.

**GREEN.**  *(A "gotcha" attitude.)* I know who you are.

**PEACOCK.**  *(Surprise.)* You do?

**GREEN.**  I work in Washington.

**PLUM.**  Washington? *(To Peacock.)* So you must be a politician's wife, Mrs. Peacock?

**PEACOCK.**  *(With renewed confidence.)* Yes, I am.

**SCARLET.**  Who's your husband? *(Cheekily.)* Maybe *I* know him.

> *Yvette reenters as dialogue continues, loudly slamming open the door, which startles the guests! Then…*

**PEACOCK.**  Mrs. White—what does *your* husband do?

**WHITE.**  Nothing.

**PLUM.**  Nothing *at all*?

**WHITE.**  Well, he just lies around on his back all day.

**SCARLET.**  *(Dryly.)* Sounds like hard work to me.

> *Thunder/lightning. Green spills his drink all over Scarlet's chest.*

**GREEN.**  *(Mopping Scarlet's chest with his napkin.)* Sorry, sorry— I'm afraid I'm a little accident-prone.

**SCARLET.**  *(Relishing his discomfort.)* Never apologize for your true nature, Mr. Green.

**GREEN.**  *(Concerned Scarlet knows more than she should.)* Sorry?

**PEACOCK.** *(Tapping him on the shoulder.)* Mr. Green—what do you do in Washington?

**GREEN.** Oh, I'd better not say. I like to follow the rules.

**PEACOCK.** *(Frustrated.)* Well, if I wasn't trying to keep the conversation going, then we would just be sitting here in an embarrassed silence.

**PLUM.** Are you afraid of silence, Mrs. Peacock?

**PEACOCK.** *(Anxiously.)* Yes. No. Why?

**PLUM.** In my professional opinion, it seems you suffer from what we call "pressure of speech."

**MUSTARD.** Is that an official diagnosis?

**WHITE.** Are you a doctor, Professor?

**PLUM.** In psychological medicine.

**WHITE.** Do you practice?

**PLUM.** *(Laced with shame.)* Not anymore.

**SCARLET.** But practice makes perfect, Professor Plum. *(Suggestively.)* I think most men need a little practice. Don't you agree, Mrs. White?

**WHITE.** *(A beat and then, deflecting.)* So what *do* you do, Professor?

**PLUM.** *(Then.)* I currently work for the government.

**WHITE.** Ah, another politician.

**PLUM.** Not exactly. I do research for U-NO WHO.

**WHITE.** *(Genuine.)* Who?

**PLUM.** *(Explaining.)* A branch of the United Nations Organization: the World—Health—Organization.

**WHITE.** *(Putting it together.)* Ahh. "U-NO WHO." *(Explaining to the table.)* It's an acronym.

**MUSTARD.** *(From the other side of the table—densely.)* I have a sister who was a gymnast.

**PLUM.** *(Flummoxed by Mustard.)* You are a *real* colonel, aren't you?

**MUSTARD.** *(Officiously.)* I am, sir.

**SCARLET.** Aren't you gonna mention the coincidence that you also live in Washington, D.C., Colonel?

**MUSTARD.** *(Deeply suspicious.)* How did you know that?

**SCARLET.** *(With a twinkle.)* Oh, I've seen you before.

**GREEN.** *(Putting it together.)* So, Miss Scarlet, does this mean that you live in Washington, too?

**SCARLET.** *(With a sly smile.)* Sure do.

**PEACOCK.** Does anyone here not live in Washington?

> *They all look at each other, putting together the coincidence.*

**PLUM.** *(Fearfully.)* Oh. Then, is this about the Red Scare?

**GREEN.** I'm not a Communist! I'm a Republican.

> *Thunder.*

> *Mustard stands, fed up.*

**MUSTARD.** Wadsworth, we've had about enough of this! Where's our host, and why have we been brought here?

> *The doorbell rings. They look out.*

**WADSWORTH.** Ah, speak of the devil. Pardon me, please.

> *Wadsworth exits through the door.*

**SCARLET.** Hey, I've got an idea.

> *Quickly Scarlet grabs her empty water glass and runs to the door.*

> *She places her ear against her glass against the door.*

> *Throughout the following dialogue, they all follow suit, lining up, single file, behind Scarlet, ears to glasses to ears of the guest in front of them, as though they are able to hear through the glass, through the ear of the guest, through the door. They talk on top of each other…*

**WHITE.** Oh yes, good thinking, Miss Scarlet.

**PEACOCK.** What are we doing?

**PLUM.** The acoustic coupling between the door and the glass allows sound waves to travel from one side to the other.

> *Once the rest are in position, poor Mustard, confused, simply stands outside the group and raises his glass to his own ear, like a real boob.*

> *We hear Wadsworth's muffled voice from the hall.*

**WADSWORTH.** All the guests have arrived as expected, sir. *(Then.)* Everything's going according to plan. *(Then.)* We'll meet you in the Study.

> *Mustard gently taps his glass, á la a microphone ("is this thing on"), to try to get it to work.*
>
> *A fraction of a moment passes and Wadsworth reenters the Dining Room from a door on the other side of the room. He clears his throat, startling the chain of guests, causing a kerfuffle. They startle, surprised at his entrance, and try to cover their faux pas.*

**ALL.** *(Ad-libbing.)* Lovely door. / Oh, hello Wadsworth, we were just playing a game. / Well, look who's back. / We didn't hear a thing. / There's a door over there?! *(Etc.)*

**PEACOCK.** *(Fed up, removing the napkin from her dress and slamming the table.)* Oh, for God's sake! Who was at the door?! I demand to know what's going on!

**WADSWORTH.** *(Evermore the butler.)* Can I interest any of you in fruit or dessert?

**ALL.** No!

**WADSWORTH.** In that case, may I suggest that we adjourn to the Study for coffee and brandy, at which point I believe your newly arrived host will reveal his intentions, your letters will be explained and…the game will be afoot.

> *Thunder/lightning! Heavy rain. As they move to the Study, transition music plays.*
>
> *Yvette and the Cook pull the table off as the Dining Room wall flies up and the Study module pushes downstage.*

## Scene 3

> *The Study.*
> *Yvette offers drinks from a bar cart.*

**YVETTE.** *(Offering.)* Coffee? Brandy?…

**WADSWORTH.** Thank you, Yvette. That will be all.

**YVETTE.** Oui, monsieur.

> *Yvette exits.*

**GREEN.** Well, where is our host?

**PEACOCK.** He's not here! Nobody's here! What is happening?!

**SCARLET.** *(Offering.)* Cigarette? It'll calm your nerves.

**PEACOCK.** I don't smoke!

> *Peacock, having pulled a flask out of her purse, takes a deep swig.*
>
> *During the above, Mustard has found a string and button-closure envelope (á la the envelope placed in the center of the Clue board game) on the desk. The envelope reads "CONFIDENTIAL" in large red letters.*

**MUSTARD.** *(Reading.)* "For Wadsworth. Open After Dinner." *(Handing it to Wadsworth.)* It's for you.

> *Wadsworth opens and reads it privately. Plum tries to get a glimpse over his shoulder.*
>
> *Wadsworth blocks his effort. A breath and then…*

**WADSWORTH.** *(Having finished.)* Right then. Are you comfortable?

**MUSTARD.** I make a good living.

**PLUM.** Oh, out with it, Wadsworth!

**WADSWORTH.** Ladies and gentlemen, these instructions are clear.

**SCARLET.** I'm glad something is.

**WADSWORTH.** It seems the six of you have all received the same letter.

> *They all reveal their letters on a music sting. Wadsworth takes the letter from Plum and reads from it.*

"It will be to your advantage to be present on this date because a Mr. Boddy will bring to end a certain long-standing confidential and painful financial liability."

**ALL.** *(Ad-libbing.)* Yes! / Yes, that's what my letter said. / Indeed! *(Etc.)*

**WADSWORTH.** As it turns out, you all have one thing in common.

**MUSTARD.** That bastard McCarthy! We're all being black*listed*, aren't we?

**WADSWORTH.** Close, Colonel.

> *Their proximity is such that Wadsworth's spit has gotten in Mustard's eye. He wipes it clean.*

You're all being black*mailed.*

> *Sinister music underscores.*

For some considerable time all of you have been paying more than you can afford to someone who threatens to expose you.

**PEACOCK.** Oh, please! What's someone going to blackmail me for? I go to church every Sunday!

**SCARLET.** Yeah lady, don't we all.

**WADSWORTH.** Anybody else wish to deny it?

> *They don't.*

Until you'd received your letters, you hadn't known *who* was blackmailing you. But now, I'm sure that even *the least discerning* amongst you has determined that the man behind your ransom… is Mr. Boddy himself.

> *Music out. They speak at once.*

**PEACOCK.** Yes, I figured as much, but who is this fellow?!

**MUSTARD.** It's Mr. Boddy? What a scoundrel!!

**WHITE.** You think I can't handle a little blackmail?!

**PLUM.** And who are you, his his henchman? You pompous, British bastard!

**GREEN.** All this stress is not good for my blood pressure!

**SCARLET.** *(Taking the reins.)* Who is this Boddy fella, you brutish butler?!

**WADSWORTH.** Who Mr. Boddy is, is no concern of yours. Suffice it to say, he's a supporter of the House Un-American Activities Committee—and he feels your *activities* have been decidedly un-American.

> *They all begin to protest…*

*(Interrupting.)* My task this evening is to expose your secrets to each other—rendering you all culpable in each others' indiscretions.

**PLUM.** But we hardly know each other.

**WADSWORTH.** Precisely.

**WHITE.**  Don't you think that you might spare us this humiliation?

**WADSWORTH.**  I'm afraid I have no choice. We'll start with you, Professor Plum.

**SCARLET.**  *(Perching on the desk.)* Oooh, this oughta be good.

**WADSWORTH.**  It says here you were once a professor of psychiatry, specializing in pathological, lying lunatics suffering from delusions of grandeur.

**PLUM.**  Yes, but now I work for the U.S. Government.

**WADSWORTH.**  So, your work has not changed. *(Then.)* But you can't practice medicine anymore, can you? Your license has been lifted, correct?

**SCARLET.**  Why? What'd he do?

**WADSWORTH.**  You know what male doctors aren't supposed to do with their lady patients?

**SCARLET.**  Yeah?

**WADSWORTH.**  Yeah, well, he did.

**PEACOCK.**  How awful! You know, someday there will be a reckoning for men like you!

**WHITE.**  I hope so.

**PEACOCK.**  *(Harshly whispered.)* You're disgusting.

**WADSWORTH.**  Are you making moral judgements, Mrs. Peacock?

**PEACOCK.**  Well, I—

**WADSWORTH.**  *(Interrupting.)* How then, do you justify taking bribes in return for delivering Senator Peacock's votes to certain lobbyists?

**PEACOCK.**  *(Defensive.)* My husband is a paid consultant. There's nothing sinful about that!

**WADSWORTH.**  Not if it's publicly declared. But if you slip cash under the men's room door at Old Ebbitt's Grill? How would you describe *that* transaction?

**SCARLET.**  I'd say it stinks.

**PEACOCK.**  *(Accusatorially.)* When were you in that men's room?

**PLUM.**  So, it's true!

**PEACOCK.** No, it's a vicious lie!

**WADSWORTH.** But you've been paying blackmail for over a year now to keep that story out of the papers. Seems a little…sticky, no?

**PEACOCK.** Now see here—

**WHITE.** *(Interrupting.)* Well, I'm willing to believe you. I too am being blackmailed for something I didn't do.

**GREEN and MUSTARD.** *(Piping up at the same moment.)* So am I.

**SCARLET.** Not me.

**WADSWORTH.** You're not being blackmailed?

**SCARLET.** Oh, I'm being blackmailed, all right. But I did what I'm being blackmailed for.

**PLUM.** What did you do?

**SCARLET.** I run my own business.

**WHITE.** That's not a crime.

**SCARLET.** You didn't ask what kind of a business I run.

**PLUM.** All right, what kind of business do you run?

**SCARLET.** I provide gentlemen with the company of a young lady.

**PEACOCK.** *(Outraged.)* An escort service?! In Washington?!

**WHITE.** How scurrilous.

**MUSTARD.** I'm sure some people are just a little lonely.

**PLUM.** *(Scoffing.)* A man who needs to pay to spend time with a woman. That's a problem I'll never have.

> *He slyly takes a business card Scarlet has pulled from her cleavage and tucks it in his coat pocket.*

**GREEN.** Is that how you knew Colonel Mustard works in Washington? Is he one of your clients?

**MUSTARD.** Certainly not!

**GREEN.** I was asking Miss Scarlet.

**MUSTARD.** *(To Scarlet.)* Well, you tell him it's not true!

**SCARLET.** "It's not true."

**PLUM.** Is that true?

**SCARLET.** No, it's not true.

**GREEN.**  Ha-hah! So it is true!

**WADSWORTH.**  A double negative!

**MUSTARD.**  Double "negative"? You mean you have—photographs?

**WADSWORTH.**  That sounds like a confession to me. In fact, the double negative has led to proof positive. I'm afraid you gave yourself away.

**MUSTARD.**  Are you trying to make me look stupid in front of the other guests?

**WADSWORTH.**  You don't need any help from me, sir.

**MUSTARD.**  That's right!

> *At just this moment, Mustard registers the insult—too late—we move on.*

**WADSWORTH.**  Colonel, looks like you hold a sensitive security post in the Pentagon. Those "negatives" would most certainly compromise your position.

**PLUM.**  *(With a wink.)* And what position exactly were you caught in, Colonel?

**MUSTARD.**  This is an outrage!

**WADSWORTH.**  *(Changing focus.)* Now, let's see, who's next?

> *He charges toward Green but spins on a dime at the last moment to…*

Mrs. White, you've been paying our friend the blackmailer ever since your husband died under, shall we say, mysterious circumstances.

**SCARLET.**  *(Laughing.)* That's why he's lying on his back all day! He's in a coffin.

**WHITE.**  Say what you want. I didn't kill him.

**MUSTARD.**  Then why are you paying the blackmailer?

**WHITE.**  I don't want another scandal, do I?

**PLUM.**  Another?

**WHITE.**  We had a very humiliating confrontation. He had threatened to kill me in public.

**SCARLET.**  Why would he want to kill you in public?

**WADSWORTH.**  I think she meant that he had threatened, in public, to kill her.

*They all react with understanding.*

**WHITE.**  It was all over the papers.

**WADSWORTH.**  And yet *he* was the one who died. Not you, Mrs. White, not you.

**WHITE.**  He was found dead at home. Unclothed. *(Then.)* But, I didn't do it. I'd been out all evening, at the movies.

**SCARLET.**  What was showing?

**WHITE.**  *The Naked Alibi.*

**SCARLET.**  A likely story.

**WADSWORTH.**  But he was your *second* husband. Your first also disappeared.

**WHITE.**  That was his job—he was an illusionist.

**WADSWORTH.**  But he never reappeared.

**WHITE.**  He wasn't a very *good* illusionist.

**WADSWORTH.**  *(Now to Green.)* And lastly, Mr. Green, who is a…

**GREEN.**  I don't need you to unmask me, Wadsworth. I know what you're gonna say about me!

**WADSWORTH.**  What's that?

**GREEN.**  "Mr. Green, who is a homosexual."

**MUSTARD.**  Not me.

**GREEN.**  I beg your pardon?

**MUSTARD.**  You asked, "Who is a homosexual," and I said, not me.

*Green and Wadsworth share a baffled moment.*

**WADSWORTH.**  Yes, thank you, Colonel. *(To Green.)* But, there's more to it than that, Mr. Green.

**GREEN.**  How do you mean?

**WADSWORTH.**  There's evidence to support the question of… your politics.

**GREEN.**  My politics?! Since when is working for the Republican party a crime?

**WADSWORTH.**  You swore an oath of allegiance to the Republican party, but neglected to vote for Eisenhower in the last election. That's grounds for an ousting if ever there was one.

**GREEN.** But voting records are confidential!

**PEACOCK.** Everything has its price, Mr. Green.

**WADSWORTH.** So—there you have it.

**PEACOCK.** *(Bordering hysteria.)* Have what?!

**WADSWORTH.** A crooked senator's wife, a lascivious doctor, a disloyal Republican, and so forth, not exactly adhering to an all-American standard of behavior, are you?

**SCARLET.** *(Knowingly.)* Depends on who you ask.

**PLUM.** But if this Boddy fella is such a noble civilian himself, then why didn't he report us to the authorities?

**WADSWORTH.** And give up the opportunity to make a buck? Come now, Professor. What could be more American than that?

**MUSTARD.** *(In earnest.)* Apple pie.

> *A collective eye roll.*

**SCARLET.** All right, Wadsworth—so we're being blackmailed by a renegade McCarthyist. Where does that leave us?

**WHITE.** Where is this Mr. Boddy?

**MUSTARD.** And what does he want from us?

**PEACOCK.** Who cares?! I'm not waiting to find out! I've done nothing wrong! I'm leaving!

> *She charges to the door.*

**WADSWORTH.** *(Blocking her efforts.)* I'm sorry, Mrs. Peacock. You can stay in denial, but you cannot leave this house!

**PEACOCK.** I am the wife of a great senator! You can't tell me what to do!

> *She tries to open the door.*

Locked?!

> *Sinister music underscores.*

**WADSWORTH.** Indeed. All the doors are locked. The windows are barred. And the grounds are patrolled by vicious dogs.

> *Dogs bark.*

There's no way out!

> *Thunder/lightning! Heavy rain. They all begin screaming at Wadsworth.*

**ALL.** *(Ad-libbing.)* Locked?! / This is an outrage! / You can't hold us hostage! / Why?! *(Etc.)*

**WADSWORTH.** *(Gaining their attention.)* Ladies and gentlemen, allow me to introduce your host for the evening, and your blackmailer for life…

> *Lightning.*

Mr. Boddy.

> *Music sting as Boddy appears in the Study doorway with confident charm.*

> *Music out.*

**BODDY.** How d'you do?

> *They speak at once.*

**PEACOCK.** Who do you think you are? I'll have you brought before Congress!

**GREEN.** Boy, would I like to give you a piece of my mind! And I don't even like confrontation!

**MUSTARD.** Bribing all these good people? I don't get it! What's in it for you?!

**PLUM.** I thought millionaires were supposed to be good-looking, you swine!

**SCARLET.** Why are you black-mailing us? I'm frustrated that I find you attractive!

**WHITE.** You're such a typical man! Better off dead!

> *White emerges at the front of the group to expertly knee Boddy in the groin.*

**SCARLET.** *(Impressed.)* Ooooh. Mrs. White, in the Study, with her knee!

**WADSWORTH.** *(Getting their attention once more.)* There is one more piece of information you may like to have.

**ALL.** What?!

**WADSWORTH.** The police are coming in less than an hour!

> *The guests react simultaneously!*

**PEACOCK.** The police? Coming here? But I'm a senator's wife. I'll be ruined!

**PLUM.** Now, let's not be rash—can't you call them off?

**SCARLET.** Oh goody. Policemen love me.

**WHITE.** This is the kind of scandal I'm trying to avoid!

**MUSTARD.** I refuse to have my record tarnished!

**GREEN.** Any idea which police department's been notified?

**BODDY.** *(Recovering/cutting them off.)* Unless…

**ALL.** Unless, what?

> *Mr. Boddy refers to his briefcase.*

**BODDY.** You agree to double down.

**SCARLET.** And why would we agree to that?

**BODDY.** Because if you don't, I'll put this briefcase—containing all the evidence needed to expose your wrongdoings—in the hands of the police, the press, and the House Un-American committee. With the right spin, those fellas can make a commie outta anyone. I think some of you would face a lifetime of jail, and others, a lifetime of shame.

**ALL.** *(Ad-libbing.)* That's why you've brought us all here?! / You bastard! / Get that briefcase! / You're taking advantage of a tenuous political situation! *(Etc.)*

**BODDY.** Unless…

**ALL.** *(Including Wadsworth.)* Unless what?!

**BODDY.** Well, there is something you could do for me that would change the game. Something I just can't bear to do myself.

**ALL.** *(Including Wadsworth.)* What?!

**BODDY.** *(To guests.)* Have a seat, please.

> *The guests move to the sofa. The ladies sit, the gentlemen stand behind. After a brief silence…*

**GREEN.** *(Re a side table behind the sofa.)* Is it all right if I sit here…

> *Before he can get the word out, Green sits on the edge of the table, which surprisingly collapses noisily.*

*(Bouncing back up.)* Sorry, sorry. Little accident-prone. Sorry.

**WADSWORTH.** *(Then—genuine to Boddy.)* What's this about, sir?

**BODDY.**  In this bag, there are six packages that I thought our guests might find useful this evening.

> *Boddy begins to empty a duffel bag full of packages into the arms of Wadsworth.*

**WADSWORTH.**  Packages?

**BODDY.**  Presents, if you will. I'm a generous sort of fellow.

**WADSWORTH.**  Are you?

**BODDY.**  Wadsworth, will you please see to it that each guest receives a gift?

**WADSWORTH.**  Gladly.

> *Wadsworth moves to distribute the gifts.*

**BODDY.** *(Pouring himself a brandy.)* Anyone wanna make a guess as to what's in your boxes?

**SCARLET.**  Perfume?

**WHITE.**  Candy?

**PEACOCK.**  A rare single-malt Scotch whiskey?

**BODDY.** *(With a laugh.)* Aren't guessing games fun? *(Then.)* Please—open them.

> *Scarlet opens her box. Puzzled, she lifts out a heavy brass Candlestick. Music sting. She looks at Boddy.*

**SCARLET.**  A Candlestick? What's this for?

> *One by one, with a music sting, each of the guests open their boxes, pulling out their "gift."*

**MUSTARD.**  A Wrench…

**GREEN.**  A Lead Pipe…

**PEACOCK.**  A Dagger…

**PLUM.**  A Revolver…

**WHITE.**  Ahhhhhh! A snake! *(Then.)* Oh, no. It's a Rope.

**BODDY.**  In your hands you each have a lethal weapon.

> *They gasp.*

You all came tonight because you believed the evidence against you was so terrible that you would do anything to keep it a secret. I'm putting that theory to the test.

**WADSWORTH.** You are?

**BODDY.** Mr. Wadsworth here is the only other person who knows your secrets, and it's costing us all dearly to keep him quiet.

**GREEN.** What do you mean?

**BODDY.** I wouldn't have to double your payments if I didn't have to pay Mr. Wadsworth for his silence.

**ALL.** Wadsworth?!

**WADSWORTH.** That's a lie!

**BODDY.** He may look suave and charming…

**WADSWORTH.** Thank you…

**BODDY.** But really he's conniving and manipulative.

**WADSWORTH.** False!

**BODDY.** Why do you think he's called the police?

**PLUM.** *(To Wadsworth.) You* called the police?

**WADSWORTH.** Only because *HE* instructed me to do so!

**BODDY.** Did I? *(Then.)* Ladies and gentlemen…if you can manage to get *rid* of Mr. Wadsworth, I'll have no need to increase your blackmail or expose you to the police.

**PLUM.** Get rid of?

**PEACOCK.** *(To White.)* Does he mean…kill him?!

**BODDY.** In fact, if you can *eliminate* Wadsworth…

**WHITE.** Yes, I think that's what he means.

**BODDY.** …Who not only knows all of your secrets, but also mine—then I will *eliminate* your blackmail altogether and be done with this terrible business once and for all.

**WADSWORTH.** You would never!

**PLUM.** But why make *us* do it, Boddy?! Why don't you do your dirty work yourself?

**GREEN.** Yeah!

**BODDY.** Why should I when the six of you are so uniquely motivated…and armed?

**SCARLET.**  What a patriot.

**WADSWORTH.**  After all I've done for you?! *(To guests.)* He's a liar! I'm one of you! I'm not a butler! I'm an indentured servant!

**BODDY.**  A familiar refrain. *(Darkly.)* Don't make a scene, Wadsworth. It's over. *(To guests.)* The police are on their way. Now's your chance. The only way for you to end your blackmail and avoid finding yourselves on the front pages is for one of you to kill Wadsworth…NOW!

> *He switches off the lights. Blackness. Chaos. Screams. A gunshot. More chaos and screams. Lights.*
>
> *Boddy lies on the floor. Prone. Face down. Everyone else is spread throughout the Study.*

**WHITE.**  It's Mr. Boddy!

**WADSWORTH.**  *(Enormously relieved.)* Oh thank God.

**SCARLET.**  Is he breathing?!

> *They rush to him in a hubbub.*

**PLUM.**  *(Cutting off the hoopla.)* Stand back, I'm a doctor!

> *They move back. Plum gives Boddy a cursory examination.*

He's dead.

**WHITE.**  Who had the gun?

**PLUM.**  I did.

**PEACOCK.**  So you shot him!

**PLUM.**  I didn't!

**PEACOCK.**  If you didn't, who did?

**PLUM.**  Somebody grabbed it from my hand, and the next thing I knew there was a shot!

> *Wadsworth turns Boddy over.*

**WADSWORTH.**  There's no gunshot wound.

**WHITE.**  He's right. There isn't.

**SCARLET.**  *(Re a hole in the wall.)* Look, there's a bullet lodged here.

**MUSTARD.**  Eagle eye, Miss Scarlet.

**GREEN.**  Well, if the bullet's over there, then how did he die over here?

**PLUM.** I don't know! I'm not a forensics expert.

**SCARLET.** Something else must have killed him.

**WHITE.** One of *us* must have killed him.

> *They all look at each other—and their weapons—nervously aware that a murderer is present amongst them.*

**GREEN.** Well, don't look at me! I didn't do it!

**ALL.** *(Joining in; ad-libbing.)* Me neither! / I didn't do it! / What're you looking at me for?! *(Etc.)*

> *Peacock, unable to find a drink elsewhere, goes to Boddy's body (who is still holding a goblet).*

**PEACOCK.** I need a drink!

> *She pries the goblet from Boddy's dead hand, raises it to her lips... She downs it just as...*

**PLUM.** Maybe Mr. Boddy was poisoned by the brandy!

> *Peacock spits out the brandy!*

**PEACOCK.** *(Screaming.)* Poison!?!

> *Peacock continues to scream. Green tries to comfort her...*

**GREEN.** There, there, Mrs. Peacock—

> *She still screams.*

I'm sure you'll be just fine—

> *She still screams.*

There's nothing to—

> *Scarlet takes over, pushing Green out of the way. She slaps Peacock, who falls onto the sofa, silenced, as the guests gasp.*

**SCARLET.** *(Offering an excuse.)* Well, someone had to stop her screaming.

**PLUM.** *(To Green.)* Was the brandy poisoned?

**GREEN.** How should I know?

**SCARLET.** Looks like now we'll never know.

**GREEN.** Unless *she* dies too.

> *They all hurry over to the sofa and stare at Peacock. Suddenly someone (Yvette) screams from another part of the house. They all look out, terror on their faces.*

*Transition music.*

**WADSWORTH.** The screams are coming from the Billiard Room!

*The guests rush out, Green has the Lead Pipe in his hand. They move to outside the Billiard Room. The Study module retreats as the Hall wall flies in.*

## Scene 4

*The Hall outside the Billiard Room.*

*Yvette's screams are louder now as Wadsworth and the guests (except Peacock) arrive at the door of the Billiard Room. Wadsworth tries the handle. The door is locked.*

**WADSWORTH.** It's locked! *(Into the door.)* Who's in there? Who's screaming?

**YVETTE.** *(From inside.)* C'est moi!

**WADSWORTH.** Yvette?!

**YVETTE.** Oui!

**WADSWORTH.** *(Into the door.)* Yvette, are you all right?!

**YVETTE.** *(From inside.)* No!

**MUSTARD.** Yvette?! Are you alive?!

*Yvette opens the door, revealing herself, in a puddle of tears, fuming!*

**YVETTE.** Of course I'm alive, you ee-diot! *(Turning to Wadsworth.)* No zanks to you—Wadsworth! You've locked us up in zis house wiz a murderer!

**WHITE.** So the murderer is here?

**YVETTE.** Oui!

**GREEN.** Where?

**YVETTE.** Where? Here! We're all looking at him.

*Peacock enters, out of breath.*

Or *her…*

**MUSTARD.**  What took you so long?

**PEACOCK.**  *(Winded and hysterical.)* I'm an old woman who may or may not have been poisoned! It's amazing I'm anywhere!

**YVETTE.**  *(Back to her point.)* I heard you all in ze Study—one of you is ze killer!

**PLUM.**  How could you hear us in "ze" Study?

**YVETTE.**  I was listening! I have a tape recorder in ze Billiard Room connected to ze Study! Monsieur Boddy asked me to record your converzation!

**PLUM.**  Why would he ask you to do that?!

**YVETTE.**  For more evidence, of course! Wadsworth revealed your secrets in ze Study; now zey are all recorded.

**PLUM.**  What a snake! I've got to destroy them! Where are the tapes?

**YVETTE.**  Who cares about ze tapes?! What about ze body?!

**MUSTARD.**  What body?

**ALL.**  Boddy's body!!

**WHITE.**  But, Yvette, why were you screaming in there, all by yourself?

**YVETTE.**  Because I was frightened! I also drank ze Cognac. Maybe I am poisoned too! *(And more to the point.)* Plus, one of you is ze killer! Monsieur Boddy is dead!

**GREEN.**  *(To Yvette.)* We have to figure out which one of *them* did it!

**PEACOCK.**  What do you mean "which one of *them*"?

**GREEN.**  Well, I didn't do it!

**WADSWORTH.**  Well, one of you did. I would have killed him myself, but I didn't have access to a weapon.

**SCARLET.**  Don't look at me! All I got was a Candlestick!

**PLUM.**  Maybe it wasn't one of us!

**GREEN.**  Who else could it have been?

**WHITE.**  Who else is in the house?

**YVETTE.**  Only ze Cook.

**ALL.** *(Looking out.)* ZE COOK!

> *Transition music as Wadsworth leads the guests to the Kitchen. The Hall wall flies out as the Kitchen module opens.*

## Scene 5

> *The Kitchen.*
>
> *They enter the Kitchen. There is a large refrigerator. Green no longer has the Lead Pipe. They look for the Cook.*

**PLUM.** As far as I can tell, the Cook's not here.

**PEACOCK.** What a lovely Kitchen. My husband and I had a Kitchen very similar to this in our first brownstone. It has such a homey feel, doesn't it…

> *As she reminisces, Green trips, accidentally causing the refrigerator door to open. The Cook's body, Dagger in her back, tumbles out onto a quite unsuspecting Green.*
>
> *Music sting. Peacock screams.*

**WHITE.** It's the Cook!

**SCARLET.** With a Dagger in her back!

**MUSTARD.** Someone must've killed her!

**GREEN.** *(Descending to the floor under the Cook's weight.)* I didn't do it!!

> *Green lands on the ground beneath the Cook. Nobody moves.*

**WADSWORTH.** This makes two.

**PLUM.** Two what?

**WADSWORTH.** Murders.

**PEACOCK.** *(Hysterical.)* I hate murders!

**MUSTARD.** I think you'd better explain yourself, Wadsworth.

**WADSWORTH.** Me?

**MUSTARD.** Well, who else would want to kill the Cook?

**SCARLET.** *(A little laugh.)* Dinner wasn't that bad.

**MUSTARD.** How can you make jokes at a time like this?

**SCARLET.** *(Defensively!)* It's my defense mechanism.

**MUSTARD.** Some defense! If I were the killer I'd kill you next.

*Everyone gasps!*

I said *"if."* There's only one admitted killer here, and it's not me. *(Pointing to White.)* It's Mrs. White!

*Everyone gasps!*

**WHITE.** I've admitted nothing.

**MUSTARD.** You paid the blackmail. How many husbands have you had?

**WHITE.** Mine or other women's?

**MUSTARD.** Yours.

**WHITE.** Five.

**MUSTARD.** Five?

**WHITE.** Yes, just the five. Husbands should be like Kleenex—soft, strong, and disposable.

**MUSTARD.** Well, if it wasn't you, who was it? Who had the Dagger?

**PLUM.** It was Mrs. Peacock!

*Everyone gasps!*

**PEACOCK.** Yes. But I put it down.

**MUSTARD.** Where?

**PEACOCK.** In the Study. Any one of us could have picked it up.

**ALL.** *(Ad-libbing.)* Well, I didn't. / It wasn't me. / I never even saw the Dagger. *(Etc.)*

**PEACOCK.** Well then, it must have been…Mr. Green!

**GREEN.** *(Under the Cook's body—muffled.)* Can somebody please help me?!

*They look, gasping!*

**WADSWORTH.** Good Lord, let him up!

**PLUM.** *(Moving to assist.)* You really oughta learn to speak up for yourself better, Mr. Green.

*Mustard and Plum lift the Cook's body off of Green. Green, gasping, recovers, getting up.*

**GREEN.** *(Breathless.)* Oh my God. Oh my God.

*Wadsworth steps over Green, who crawls away (perhaps taking a swig from Peacock's flask), as dialogue continues.*

**WADSWORTH.** Gentlemen, might I suggest we take the Cook's body into the Study.

*Wadsworth hoists the Cook out of Mustard and Plum's arms and onto his back.*

**SCARLET.** Why?

**WADSWORTH.** Well, for starters, when the police arrive, if they find this…

*He dumps the Cook's body off his back and into the arms of the rest of the group.*

…We'll all be in custody and under suspicion for murder.

**PEACOCK.** Murder!

**WADSWORTH.** And secondly, I'm the butler. I like to keep the Kitchen tidy.

*They heave-ho, grumbling as they do, puppeteering the Cook's body from the Kitchen back to the Study to transition music as the Kitchen module retreats and the Study module returns to position.*

### Scene 6

*The Study.*

*To the tail end of transition music, the guests, except Wadsworth, enter. They stop and slowly look back to the spot where Boddy was. HE'S GONE!*

**PLUM.** The body's gone!

*They freeze! They drop the Cook to the ground with a thud! Just then, Wadsworth enters, breathless.*

**WADSWORTH.**  What are you all staring at?

**PLUM.**  Nobody.

**WADSWORTH.**  What do you mean?

**PEACOCK.**  *(Panic-stricken.)* Nobody. No body. Mr. Boddy's body. It's gone!

**WHITE.**  Maybe he wasn't really dead.

**PLUM.**  He was!

**WHITE.**  We should have made sure.

**PLUM.**  I thought I had!

**MUSTARD.**  So was he dead or wasn't he?

**GREEN.**  Maybe he was dead, but someone moved him!

**SCARLET.**  Who would move him?

**WHITE.**  And why?!

**GREEN.**  How should I know?!

**PLUM.**  Well, if he's not here—then where is he?

**PEACOCK.**  Oh my. All this excitement. If you'll excuse me, I have to uh…is there a little girl's room?

**YVETTE.**  Oui oui, madame.

**PEACOCK.**  *(Misunderstanding.)* No, I just want to powder my nose.

**YVETTE.**  Zere's a toilette outside ze Billiard Room.

  *Peacock exits.*

**WADSWORTH.**  *(Clocking Peacock's exit.)* Uhhhh… *(Then.)* I don't mean to alarm anybody, but we do currently have the small issue of two dead bodies: one missing, one present—and the imminent arrival of the police…

**SCARLET.**  The bridge is washed out; that should buy us some extra time.

**YVETTE.**  But I don't want extra time! I want ze polize to arrive! I am trapped in zis houze wiz a murderer!

**PLUM.**  But once the police get here, the rest of us are doomed.

**GREEN.**  We'll all go to the chair!

**MUSTARD.**  *(Taking charge.)* Wadsworth, am I right in thinking that there is nobody else in this house?

**WADSWORTH.** Um, no.

**MUSTARD.** Then there is someone else in this house?

**WADSWORTH.** Sorry, I said "no" meaning "yes."

**MUSTARD.** "No" meaning "yes"?

**WADSWORTH.** Yes.

**MUSTARD.** Look, I want a straight answer.

**GREEN.** Don't look at me.

> *They look at him.*

**MUSTARD.** There seems to be some confusion about whether or not we are the only people in this house.

**WADSWORTH.** There isn't.

**MUSTARD.** There isn't any confusion or there isn't anybody else?

**WADSWORTH.** Either. Both.

**MUSTARD.** Just give me a clear answer! Is there anyone else in the house?

**ALL.** No!

**MUSTARD.** Know with a silent K or…

**SCARLET.** *(Cutting him off.)* Look, we've got a killer on the loose, the missing dead body of Mr. Boddy, a Cook with a Dagger in her back, and all these easily accessible weapons—the Rope, the Revolver, the Candlestick, the Wrench—and—hey, where's the Lead Pipe?

> *Music sting. Peacock screams. She enters, stumbling into the room with Boddy hanging all over her. It looks like Boddy is attacking her.*

**PLUM.** It's Mr. Boddy!

**GREEN.** He's attacking her.

> *While Peacock continues her hysteria, the bloodied Boddy falls off of her and onto the ground. The Lead Pipe protrudes from his skull.*

*(Grossed out.)* Oh God, he's so bloody!

**PLUM.** Stand back! *(Completing a second cursory exam.)* He's dead.

**SCARLET.** That's what you said the last time.

**PLUM.** I believe in second chances.

**WADSWORTH.** Mr. Boddy? Dead? *Again?*

**PEACOCK.** I'm going to faint!

**WADSWORTH.** I'll catch you!

> *Peacock collapses in Wadsworth's arms. He releases her and she falls back with a thud.*

Sorry.

**WHITE.** Mrs. Peacock?

**PEACOCK.** *(Popping up, woozy.)* Yes?

**WHITE.** Where did this happen?

**PEACOCK.** *(From the ground.)* In the bathroom! I opened the door and there he was! At first, I thought he was attacking me, but then I realized he'd been left propped up against the doorframe, dead, just waiting to fall on someone!

> *Perhaps she pulls a tiny bottle of booze out from her cleavage and downs it while…*

**WHITE.** Who would do such a thing?

**PLUM.** Takes a lotta guts to kill someone twice.

**SCARLET.** It's what we call overkill.

**GREEN.** But why?!

**PLUM.** What's the difference?

**SCARLET.** Makes a difference to him!

**WADSWORTH.** *(Losing it.)* Makes a difference to us! We've got to find out *who* killed him, *where*, and *with what*!

> *Referencing the Lead Pipe in Boddy's head.*

**PLUM.** Seems like it was probably the Lead Pipe.

**WADSWORTH.** Ten points, Professor Plum.

**MUSTARD.** What kind of game are you playing, Wadsworth?

**WADSWORTH.** This isn't a game!

**PLUM.** *(To Green.)* You! The Lead Pipe belonged to you!

**GREEN.** But I dropped it while running to the Kitchen!

**PLUM.** People don't just drop murder weapons!

**GREEN.** I didn't know it was a murder weapon when I dropped it!

**WHITE.** So anyone could have picked it up?

**WADSWORTH.** *(Becoming unhinged.)* Yes of course, but who did?!? Who did pick up the Lead Pipe? Who picked up the Lead Pipe and brutally murdered Mr. Boddy, leaving him dead and bloodied in the bathroom? Who did that? Who?! Who?!?! Who?!?!?!

**SCARLET.** *(From the desk.)* Cool it, Butler! While you lose your marbles, I'm over here trying to do something useful! Have you all forgotten about the evidence against us?

**ALL.** The evidence!

> *They move toward Scarlet. Scarlet tries to open Boddy's briefcase.*

**SCARLET.** Boddy's briefcase is locked.

**WHITE.** There must be a key!

**WADSWORTH.** Mr. Green, would you be so kind as to check Mr. Boddy's pockets for the key to his briefcase containing the evidence of our crimes, so that we may destroy said evidence once and for all?

**GREEN.** Why me?

**WADSWORTH.** Why not?

**GREEN.** *(Unhappily.)* Well…all right.

> *He pulls out a latex glove, putting it on.*

**SCARLET.** Where'd you get that?

**GREEN.** I don't like germs.

**SCARLET.** Or fingerprints?

**GREEN.** No, mostly it's really just germs.

> *Green searches Boddy's pocket, gagging/holding back vomit.*

*(With his hand in Boddy's pocket—gagging.)* Oh God, it's so warm. *(Then.)* Aha! Got it!

**SCARLET.** Give it here!

> *He rushes it over to Scarlet, who opens the briefcase.*

It's empty!

> *They gasp!*

**WADSWORTH.**  Empty?!

**MUSTARD.**  Then where's all the evidence?

**WADSWORTH.**  I told you Boddy was a liar! Had the evidence in his briefcase, my foot!

**GREEN.**  We must find that evidence!

**SCARLET.**  And destroy it!

**MUSTARD.**  *(Becoming officious.)* Evidence against us aside, first things first. We're in a room with two dead bodies.

**YVETTE.**  And ze cops are on zeir way!

**MUSTARD.**  Let's move the corpses to the couch so they look less dead.

> *They do. What follows is a farcical moving of the two dead bodies from the floor onto the sofa.*

**PLUM.**   *(Immediately—stepping over the Cook to get to Boddy.)* Some party this is turning out to be.

**YVETTE.**  *(Crossing to the Cook.)* Help me, Monsieur Green.

**GREEN.**  *(Dubious.)* Well, all right.

> *Yvette and Green drag the Cook, while Plum drags Boddy.*

**WADSWORTH.**  Careful. Don't get guts on the ground.

**MUSTARD.**  *(Impressed by Plum dragging Boddy's body.)* Solid battlefield technique, Professor Plum. Never leave a man behind.

**WHITE.**  Cadavers are heavier than they seem, aren't they?

**WADSWORTH.**  I wouldn't know.

**WHITE.**  Right. Me neither.

**GREEN.**  *(Lifting Boddy up.)* Upsy-daisy.

**WHITE.**  *(Then re the Cook.)* Here, prop her up.

**PEACOCK.**  *(From her unhelpful perch on the desk.)* Aren't you all strong and virile?

> *She drinks from a flask.*
>
> *The guests ad-lib appropriately until the bodies are both in position on the sofa with Green, writhing, pinned between them.*

*Green, gagging, unpins himself, escaping the sofa. The guests prop both bodies (Dagger and Lead Pipe fully visible) upright.*

**WHITE.**  Good. They just look asleep.

**SCARLET.**  Forget about the bodies! We need to do something about this room full of murder weapons and the homicidal maniac on the loose!

**WADSWORTH.**  Let's put the weapons in the bag!

*Wadsworth starts to put the remaining weapons in Boddy's bag.*

**SCARLET.**  What good will that do?

**WADSWORTH.**  Then we'll zip up the bag.

**WHITE.**  Most murderers know how zippers work, Mr. Wadsworth.

**WADSWORTH.**  I know! We'll put the bag in the safe!

**SCARLET.**  Terrific! *(Looking all around.)* Where's the safe?

**WADSWORTH.**  In the Hall!

*Transition music. As the Study module retreats, the Hall wall flies in as they move to the Hall.*

Shush.

*They stop. Listen. More transition music as they move again.*

## Scene 7

*The Hall.*

*They arrive and Wadsworth tinkers with the bottom of a large framed portrait hanging between two doors.*

**SCARLET.**  I don't see a safe.

**PLUM.**  *(Re the art.)* Is that an original Trumbull, Mr. Wadsworth?

**WHITE.**  Those are quite valuable.

**PEACOCK.**  Now is not the time for art appreciation! *(Then.)* Butler…

*Before Peacock can finish her thought, Wadsworth opens the painting on the wall to reveal a safe.*

**ALL GUESTS.**  *(Gently impressed.)* Ohhh.

> *As Wadsworth throws the bag in and locks the "painting"…*

**MUSTARD.**  A hidden safe behind a portrait. *(Wildly earnest.)* How original!

**WADSWORTH.**  There! Locked!

**YVETTE.**  Voilá!

**MUSTARD.**  What are you going to do with the key to the safe, Wadsworth?

**YVETTE.**  Oh yes! Ze key!

**WADSWORTH.**  I'll put it in my pocket.

**PEACOCK.**  But what if you're the murderer?

**WADSWORTH.**  I'm not.

**PEACOCK.**  But what if you are?

**WADSWORTH.**  I've an idea—we'll throw it outside.

**YVETTE.**  Oui! A l'extérieur!

**PEACOCK.**  But it's raining "a l'extérieur!"

**WADSWORTH.**  I'm not suggesting *we* go outside. I'm suggesting we stay *inside*, but throw away the key.

**PLUM.**  *(Warily.)* But you'd have to open the door, wouldn't you?

**WADSWORTH.**  I would.

**PLUM.**  But what if the killer is outside?

**GREEN.**  Better out than in!

**PLUM.**  Yes! We'd want to keep him outside, wouldn't we? If we open the door we risk letting him back in.

**WHITE.**  But maybe, if we open the door, we'd encourage the killer to go out!

**SCARLET.**  The killer seems to be doing a fine job of opening and closing doors all by himself. I don't see how us opening the door for one tiny second could possibly make any sort of a difference.

**MUSTARD.**  But what if we open the door, throw away the key, and the killer catches it. Then the killer would have the key we're trying to confiscate!

**WADSWORTH.** We might be overthinking this. *(Then.)* I'm going to throw away the key. Follow me.

> *Transition music as the guests run toward the front door as the Hall wall flies up.*

## Scene 8

> *The Front Door.*
>
> *Wadsworth leads Yvette and the guests toward the front door. He opens the door to throw away the safe key, but shockingly, a motorist stands at the door, poised to knock. The guests scream.*

**WADSWORTH.** *(Screaming.)* Not now!

> *Wadsworth slams the door in the Motorist's face. The guests are breathless with fear.*

**GREEN.** Was that the killer?!

**WHITE.** He didn't look like a killer.

**PLUM.** *(A dig.)* Takes one to know one.

**MUSTARD.** Leave him to me. Interrogation is my speciality.

> *Mustard opens the door.*

How do you do?

**MOTORIST.** I'm sorry… *(As he enters, searching for words.)* I didn't mean to disturb the whole household, but my car broke down out here, and I was wondering if I could use your phone.

**MUSTARD.** *(Accusatorially.)* Are you a killer?

**MOTORIST.** What? No!

**MUSTARD.** *(Entirely convinced.)* All right then. This way please.

> *He shows him in as the others start to protest…*

**MOTORIST.** Thank you.

> *He steps fully into the mansion.*

Well? Where is it?

**MUSTARD.** What? The body?

*The others gasp!*

**MOTORIST.** The phone. *(Realizing.)* What body?

**WADSWORTH.** What? There's no body. There's nobody.

**MUSTARD.** Riiiight. There's nobody in the Study.

> *Mustard has inadvertently pointed to the Study. The Motorist starts walking toward it. Everyone realizes that's where the bodies are!*

**ALL.** *(Preventing him from going to the Study.)* No!!!

**WADSWORTH.** No, no, that phone's dead…*disconnected.* But I think there's one in the Lounge.

**MOTORIST.** Alrighty then.

> *Wadsworth brings the Motorist to the door of the Lounge as the others look on.*

**WADSWORTH.** Right through this door.

**MOTORIST.** Thank you.

> *Wadsworth opens the door, lets the Motorist in. Closes and locks the door. Mustard has simultaneously poked his head into the Study so that as Wadsworth turns around he notices…*

**WADSWORTH.** Everything all right?

**MUSTARD.** *(Shutting the door behind him.)* Yep. Two corpses. Everything's fine.

**WADSWORTH.** *(To guests with renewed, intense urgency.)* Now listen…we haven't much time. Our task is twofold. ONE: Find the evidence! TWO: Find the murderer!

**PLUM.** We've got one potential suspect contained in the Lounge—but that leaves the whole rest of this place up for grabs. Who knows what's behind all these doors.

**MUSTARD.** I suggest we handle this in proper military fashion. We split up and search the house.

**PEACOCK.** Split up?!

**MUSTARD.** Yes! We'll split up into pairs. That way none of us will be alone.

**PLUM.** But if we split up into pairs, whichever one of us is paired with the killer might get killed!

**YVETTE.** Mon dieu!

**MUSTARD.** But then we would have discovered who the murderer is!

**PEACOCK.** But the other half of the pair would be dead!

**MUSTARD.** This is war, Peacock! Casualties are inevitable. You cannot make an omelette without breaking eggs—every cook will tell you that.

**PEACOCK.** But look what happened to the Cook!

**GREEN.** Colonel, are you willing to take that chance?

**MUSTARD.** What choice do we have?

**SCARLET.** None.

**GREEN.** I suppose you're right.

**MUSTARD.** *(Officious.)* All right, troops. Divide and conquer. I'll split us into pairs. *(Now childish.)* One potato, two potato, three pota...

**WADSWORTH.** *(Interrupting, completing the rhyme.)* No more! *(Then taking the reins.)* Mrs. White, you come with me. Professor Plum, you're with Mrs. Peacock. Yvette, you go with Mr. Green; and Miss Scarlet, you're with Mr. Potato Head.

**PEACOCK.** But what if someone doesn't come back?

**WADSWORTH.** We'll remember you fondly. Now, leave no door unopened. And...cherish your partner. This might be the last person you ever see.

 *They go!*

# Scene 9


*The Hall.*

*The pairs search the house through an elaborate musical montage of choreographed, door-slamming tomfoolery, punctuated by brief vignettes.*

*After an initial series of highly stylized crosses and door openings, the Hall wall flies in and the focus shifts to White and Wadsworth, now alone in the Hall, facing two doors.*

**WHITE.**  Go on. I'll be right behind you.

**WADSWORTH.**  That's why I'm nervous.

**WHITE.**  But why? It's just us. We're alone.

**WADSWORTH.**  That's just it, Mrs. White. No man in his right mind would ever be alone with you.

**WHITE.**  Fine. You go in there and I'll go in here.

*They go to two doors. They don't go in.*

Are you going in?

**WADSWORTH.**  Yes, are you?

**WHITE.**  Yes.

*They fake each other out three times in quick succession. Then…*

**WADSWORTH.**  On the count of three. (*A beat and then.*) One… Three!

*Wadsworth and White enter and exit their respective rooms abruptly.*

**WHITE.**  Nothing in that room.

**WADSWORTH.**  Nothing in that room either.

**WHITE.**  Shall we search the Ballroom?

**WADSWORTH.**  (*Gesturing for her to go first.*) After you.

*White and Wadsworth's stylized movement leads them into an elaborate tango that plays as they exit.*

*As the Hall wall flies out, the guests crisscross the entry Hall, causing each other to startle.*

*Mustard and Scarlet meet in the middle, each holding a notepad and tiny golf pencil (from the Clue board game). They compare their notes and each exit separately as the Library module slides into place.*

*Focus shifts to Peacock and Plum in the Library.*

**PLUM.** *(Seated in an armchair.)* This is quite an impressive Library.

**PEACOCK.** How can I find anything if I don't even know what I'm looking for!

**PLUM.** *(Reading from a book.)* "Civilized society is perpetually menaced with disintegration through this primary hostility of men towards one another."

**PEACOCK.** Your fancy words don't intimidate me, Professor!

**PLUM.** I take no credit, Mrs. Peacock. *(Re the book.)* Freud. I think he's onto something.

**PEACOCK.** *(Taking the book from him.)* Now is not the time for academic pursuits! We're supposed to find the evidence!

*Peacock puts the book back in the bookshelf, triggering an elaborate, FBI-style secret panel labeled "EVIDENCE," plastered with headshots (in the style of the Clue game cards) and notes detailing the guests' crimes to flip and appear in the wall directly behind them. They do not see it as they carry on.*

**PLUM.** It's a fruitless search if you ask me. I mean, it's not like we're gonna find the evidence plastered on a wall somewhere.

**PEACOCK.** I suppose you're right.

**PLUM.** C'mon, let's go upstairs. Maybe we'll be excited by something in a bedroom.

**PEACOCK.** *(Uncharacteristically delighted.)* Ooooh! I haven't been excited by something in a bedroom for years!

*Disgusted, Plum exits, with Peacock, giddy, hot on his trail.*

*Lights shift as the module retreats.*

*The guests crisscross once more, featuring an unexpected,*

**MOTORIST.** I'm a little nervous. I'm at that big house on the hill, and I've been locked in the Lounge. I didn't expect there'd be a whole group of people here—I think they're having some sort of party; and the funny thing is, I think one of them is my customer.

*As he's talking, the portrait behind him opens and a gloved hand appears behind him with a raised Wrench...*

Yeah, my regular Tuesday night passenger...

*The Wrench comes down on the Motorist's head. Blackout. The Lounge retreats.*

*Search music continues as the Conservatory wall flies in and the lights shift to find Scarlet and Mustard in the Conservatory.*

## Scene 10

*The Conservatory.*

*Mustard searches the Conservatory floor. Scarlet enters slyly, holding Plum's pipe.*

**SCARLET.** *(Whispering conspiratorially.)* Psst!

*Mustard yelps, startled!*

**MUSTARD.** Oh, there you are.

**SCARLET.** You'll never believe what I found in the hallway? *(Showing.)* Professor Plum's stupid tobacco pipe!

**MUSTARD.** Huh. What do you think that means?

**SCARLET.**  Who knows! But it seems suspicious if you ask me.

**MUSTARD.**  I just did.

**SCARLET.**  Honest to God, Colonel.

**MUSTARD.**  Hey—what room is this anyway?

**SCARLET.**  Search me.

**MUSTARD.**  *(Frisking her.)* All right.

**SCARLET.**  Hey! Get your mitts off me! It's just an expression!

**MUSTARD.**  My apologies, Miss Scarlet. I struggle with nuance.

**SCARLET.**  *(Moving on.)* This is the last room left to search in this beastly mansion and we still haven't found the evidence.

**MUSTARD.**  I think this time has been productive nevertheless.

**SCARLET.**  Aren't you a Pollyanna.

**MUSTARD.**  You're a brave and determined lady, Miss Scarlet. I've really enjoyed our time together. I hope after this expedition ends we can remain friends.

> *Scarlet continues intensely searching.*

I mean, really, murders aside, it's just been a lovely group of people all in all. I suppose I would like to hear Mrs. White explain when and how she lost her veil in the Billiard Room, but…

**SCARLET.**  *(Grabbing the veil.)* You found White's veil in the Billiard Room? Odd.

**MUSTARD.**  Odd?

**SCARLET.**  Odd.

> *Mustard accidentally leans on the wall sconce, which moves like a lever.*
>
> *A trap door opens.*

*(Gasp.)* A trap door! *(Then.)* A trap door leading to a secret passage! C'mon!

**MUSTARD.**  *(Clearing his throat.)* Uh… Ladies first, Miss Scarlet.

**SCARLET.**  *(Rolling her eyes.)* How heroic.

> *Scarlet steps into the passage; Mustard follows her. Blackout as music continues. The Conservatory wall flies up as the Lounge module opens.*

<h1 style="text-align:center">Scene 11</h1>

*The Lounge.*

*The painting opens and (auxiliary) Scarlet and Mustard climb out of it. The room is dark. The dead Motorist in the chair is unnoticed…for now.*

*Please note: Scarlet and Mustard are substituted by an auxiliary man and woman dressed as Scarlet and Mustard. The lighting is such that we can't see their faces and the real Scarlet and Mustard continue their dialogue from offstage or via prerecorded voice-over.*

**MUSTARD.**  Where are we now?

**SCARLET.**  How should I know? The lights are off.

**MUSTARD.**  Well turn them on!

**SCARLET.**  I would if I could see anything!

**MUSTARD.**  Well I'm going to feel my way around.

**SCARLET.**  Don't get any funny ideas.

**MUSTARD.**  *(Feeling.)* A table…

**SCARLET.**  *(Feeling.)* A telephone…

**MUSTARD.**  A chair…

**SCARLET.**  A body…

*Scarlet and Mustard stop dead in their tracks.*

**SCARLET and MUSTARD.**  A body!!! Ahhhhhh!!!!!!!!!!!!!!!!!

*Music sting.*

**SCARLET.**  Find the door!

**MUSTARD.**  Get me out of here!

*They find the door but the door is locked.*

**SCARLET and MUSTARD.**  HELP! HELP! MURDER! MURDER!

*The stage is now divided in two, with inside the Lounge being stage left, and outside the Lounge being stage right. The guests scurry toward the Lounge from all over the house, ad-libbing, as they make their way to the door—realizing*

**ALL GUESTS.** LET US IN! LET US IN!

**SCARLET and MUSTARD.** *(Voices.)* LET US OUT! LET US OUT!

**WADSWORTH.** We can't let you out! The door to the Lounge is locked!

**SCARLET.** *(Through the door.)* You had the key, Wadsworth! You locked the Motorist in here!

**WADSWORTH.** That's right! I did! I do! *(Checking his pockets.)* I don't! The keys are gone!

**ALL.** Gone?!

**YVETTE.** I have an idea!

*Yvette runs offstage.*

**SCARLET.** *(Through the door.)* There's a murderer on the loose! Please get us out of here!

*Plum walks back from the door, at his most macho.*

**PLUM.** There's no alternative. I'm just gonna have to break down the door. *(To the others.)* Stand back! I'm a doctor!

*Just as he backs up to prepare to run, Yvette runs onstage holding the gun.*

**YVETTE.** Stand back! I'm a woman!

*Plum backs into Yvette. Their crash causes her gun to go off, firing upwards. The chandelier above—in slo-mo—falls, pinning Green beneath it as the guests react (also in slo-mo)!*

**GREEN.** *(In slo-mo via V.O.)* Can somebody please help me?

*We restore to regular speed. All the guests scream as Green rolls out from beneath the chandelier that nearly crushed him!*

**SCARLET and MUSTARD.** *(Through the door; ad-libbing.)* What happened?! / What was that?! / Help! Murder! Help! *(Etc.)*

**YVETTE.** I will help you!

*Yvette, still determined to save the day, points the gun to the*

*Lounge door. With surprising expertise, she fires the gun twice at the lock.*

I'm done shooting at you! Ze door is open! You can come out now!

*The real Mustard and Scarlet exit the Lounge.*

**MUSTARD.** *(Angrily, to Yvette.)* Why were you shooting at us?

**YVETTE.** To open ze door!

**MUSTARD.** But you could have killed us!

**YVETTE.** *(Defensively.)* I said "stand back"!

**MUSTARD.** *(To Wadsworth.)* Let's add "finding the key to the Lounge" to our priority list.

**PLUM.** Say, Frenchy—where did you get that gun anyway?

**YVETTE.** Ze zafe. It was unlocked!

**ALL.** Unlocked!?!?

**WADSWORTH.** Impossible! I have the key! *(Checking his pocket.)* No I haven't! It's gone!

**ALL.** Gone?!

**MUSTARD.** Not to beat a dead horse, but, again, I feel like having all the keys is really— *(Important.)*

**PLUM.** *(Interrupting.)* I thought you said you'd throw away the key to the safe, Wadsworth!

**WADSWORTH.** I did say that! But I didn't do that! We got distracted by the Motorist at the door and I forgot. One of you must have snatched the keys from my pocket when we were searching the house.

**PLUM.** So whoever took the keys, is the killer.

**WADSWORTH.** Precisely.

**SCARLET.** Speaking of the killer, there's a dead body in the Lounge, ya know! The Motorist is dead!

*She opens the Lounge door. Music sting. They all peek in.*

**PEACOCK.** Which one of you killed him?

**SCARLET.** *(Outraged.)* We found him, together!

**MUSTARD.** And he was already dead!

**GREEN.** But the door to the Lounge was locked!

**SCARLET.** We went through a secret passage we found in the Conservatory.

**PLUM.** A secret passage?! Who designed this place?

**WADSWORTH.** The Parker Brothers.

> *The doorbell rings. They look out and gasp. They stand still, frozen in terror.*
>
> *They wait. And hope. Doorbell again. They look to the front door. Doorbell rings a third time. They huddle, worrying aloud.*

**ALL.** *(Ad-libbing.)* What should we do? / Let's hide! / Shhh! / You're being too loud! / Maybe this time it's the killer! *(Etc.)*

**PLUM.** *(Within the melee, taking the gun from Yvette and stashing it on his body.)* Quick! I'll hide the gun!

> *KNOCK KNOCK KNOCK.*

**WADSWORTH.** Don't worry, it's not the police.

**COP.** It's the police!

> *Everyone gasps!*

**GREEN.** I'm going to open the door.

**ALL.** No!

**GREEN.** I've nothing to hide. I didn't do it!

> *He runs up to the front door, the guests at his heels.*

**COP.** Open the door!

> *Green opens the front door. A Cop stands there.*

Good evening, sir.

**GREEN.** Good evening, Officer. We've been expecting you.

**COP.** You have?

**GREEN.** We haven't?

**COP.** I got a tip about an abandoned car near the gates of this house. Did a motorist stop by for help, by any chance?

> *They try to smooth away his suspicions.*

**ALL.** No.

**GREEN.** *(On the heels of "No"—compelled to tell the truth.)* Yes.

**COP.** *(Skeptically.)* There seems to be some disagreement. At any rate, can I come in and use the phone?

**ALL.** No!

**GREEN.** Of course you may, sir. There's a phone in the Lounge.

> *Scarlet, who is closest to the Lounge door, blocks it.*

**SCARLET.** Out of order.

**GREEN.** Of course. My mistake. You can use the phone in the Study.

> *Plum, who is closest to the Study door, blocks it.*

**PLUM.** Occupied.

**GREEN.** Uhhh…

**WADSWORTH.** *(Taking over.)* If you please, sir, you may use the phone in the Library. Right this way.

**COP.** You're all acting rather peculiar.

**WADSWORTH.** It's because our chandelier fell down.

**ALL.** *(Ad-libbing.)* Yes. / Exactly. / That's true. / We loved that chandelier. *(Etc.)*

**WADSWORTH.** It could have killed us. But don't worry, the maid will clean it up.

**COP.** That's all well and good, but…what's going on in the Lounge and Study?

**WADSWORTH.** Lounging. Studying. This way…

**COP.** Let me have a look.

**WADSWORTH.** No thank you.

**COP.** What?

**WADSWORTH.** *(Deflective.)* Hm? *(Then.)* This way, please.

**COP.** Actually, I'd like to take a look around if you don't mind.

**WADSWORTH.** Of course, Officer. *(Forcibly walking him down stage—slowly.)* Follow me. I'll take you on a grand tour of Boddy Manor.

> *Simultaneously, the guests huddle up, quietly whispering together to come up with a plan, while Yvette uses a pulley system by the front door to raise the chandelier back into position.*

This home was built by Lord Reginald Boddy in 1784… *(Ushering him through.)* This way please.

**SCARLET.**  We've got to cover our tracks and get rid of this guy!

**WADSWORTH.**  *(Distracting him.)* Lord *Boddy* had been declared Lord *Boddy* after some*body* discovered an anti*body* that would save every*body*.

> *White, Peacock, Mustard, and Yvette head to the Study where Boddy and the Cook's bodies remain.*

> *Plum, Scarlet, and Green head to the Lounge where the Motorist's body remains.*

*(Desperately trying to distract—he drops to the floor—nearly singing/ doing snow angels.)* Notice the mahogany floor. *(Then—vibrantly.)* Did you know, in the 17th century, the buccaneer John Esquemeling recorded the use of mahogany for making canoes? *(Mimes rowing a canoe.)* Can you canoe?

**COP.**  *(Baffled.)* What?

> *The two groups have each entered their respective rooms. The Cop turns around to find the stage bare.*

Hey—where'd everybody go?

**WADSWORTH.**  *(Continuing his desperate tour.)* Notice the brass doorknobs. Crafted specifically for Lord *Boddy* by his *buddy* in 1878—

**COP.**  *(Irritated.)* I don't care about the doorknobs, Mister! What's going on around here? What are you hiding in those two rooms?!

**WADSWORTH.**  *(Trying to cover.)* Uh…which two rooms?

**COP.**  The Lounge and the Study!

**WADSWORTH.**  Oh… Oh. Ohhhhh. Those two rooms—

**COP.**  Yes!

> *Cop approaches the Study door. Wadsworth blocks his path.*

**WADSWORTH.**  No! No! NO! Officer, I don't think you should go in there.

**COP.**  Why not?

**WADSWORTH.**  Because it's…all too shocking!

> *Cop shoves Wadsworth aside as a Study module opens. As*

*the Cop enters, the guests puppeteer the dead bodies of Boddy and the Cook so they appear to be alive.*

*We hear 1950s rock-and-roll on the radio.*

*Yvette dusts the furniture to the beat of the music. She waves flirtatiously at Cop.*

**YVETTE.**  Hello, Officer! Welcome to ze party!

*White has set herself up with the dead body of Boddy on top of her, to make it appear as if they're making out.*

*Cop walks past them, embarrassed.*

**COP.**  Excuse me.

*Yvette dusts him.*

**YVETTE.**  You are excuzed!

*Cop now notices Mustard seemingly making out with the dead Cook, while Peacock, unseen by Cop behind drapes, uses her hands as if they were the Cook's hands, heavily petting Mustard.*

**COP.**  Pardon me.

*Cop moves to exit. Yvette calls after him.*

**YVETTE.**  Good night, Officer.

**COP.**  Good night!

*SLAM! Cop retreats from the Study back into the main Hall with Wadsworth.*

*As the Study module retreats, the guests react in disgust as they pull away from the dead bodies.*

That wasn't all that shocking, mister. Those folks were just having a good time. Why didn't you tell me this was a party?

**WADSWORTH.**  My…apologies sir.

**COP.**  I'll just take a peek in the Lounge, if you don't mind.

*Cop has crossed the Hall to the Lounge and opens the door as the Lounge module opens.*

*We hear a different rock-and-roll song on a record player.*

*The dead Motorist, an alcohol bottle in hand, appears to be drunk rather than dead. He is propped up in a chair, by*

*Green, who shares the chair with him, also pretending to be drunk. Plum and Scarlet are slow dancing to the music behind him.*

*(Speaking into the doorway.)* Excuse me?

**GREEN.**  *(Slurring his words.)* Ev'ning Officer. How d'ya do.

**COP.**  Are these men drunk?

**SCARLET.**  Dead drunk.

**GREEN.**  *(Offering booze from Boddy's limp hand—splashing booze everywhere.)* Wanna sip?

**COP.**  Oh, I can't drink while on the job. The Chief would kill me.

**GREEN.**  Killed if you do, killed if you don't…

**COP.**  What?

**GREEN.**  Huh?

**COP.**  *(To Boddy.)* I hope you're not going to drive home tonight?

**PLUM.**  Oh, he won't be driving home, Officer. We'll get a car for him.

**SCARLET.**  A long, black car.

**PLUM.**  Have a lovely evening, Officer.

**COP.**  *(With a tip of his hat.)* Same to you.

> *Cop shuts the door. As the Lounge module retreats, Scarlet and Plum help Green, disgusted, out of the chair. Green, hyperventilating, breathes into his latex glove (inflating it again and again) as the Lounge module closes.*

Well…

**WADSWORTH.**  *(With slight desperation.)* I can explain everything.

**COP.**  No explanation necessary. There's nothing illegal about any of this.

**WADSWORTH.**  There's not?

**COP.**  Of course not! This is America—it's a free country, ya know.

**WADSWORTH.**  I didn't know it was *that* free.

**COP.**  May I use your phone now?

**WADSWORTH.**  Certainly!

> *Wadsworth leads Cop to the Library.*

*(Opening the door.)* The Library, Officer.

**COP.** Thank you.

 *Wadsworth closes and locks the door behind him. Then…*

**WADSWORTH.** *(Nearly whispered.)* All's clear! You can come out now. Well done, all of you. Impressive!

 *All the guests emerge into the Hall congratulating themselves.*

**ALL.** *(Ad-libbing.)* You really pulled that off! / Nice touch with the alcohol bottle. / I didn't know you had it in you. *(Etc.)*

**WADSWORTH.** *(Gaining their attention.)* Psst! *(Then.)* All right, I've locked him in the Library…

**SCARLET.** How'd you do that? I thought you didn't have the keys!

**WADSWORTH.** I didn't have my right-pocket keys. *(Revealing keys from his other pocket.)* But my left-pocket keys are in tact. *(Then.)* Now—let's finish searching the Manor! The police are on their way!

**PLUM.** But, the police already came!

**GREEN.** Not the "broken-down car" police, the "criminal investigation" police.

**WADSWORTH.** Precisely. *(Then.)* We must find the evidence and we can't afford to have any more murders! This is getting dangerous. Now go!

 *Transition music. The guests disperse to search the house! Both the Library module and the Billiard Room module push on.*

## Scene 12

 *The Library/The Billiard Room.*

 *The Cop dials the phone. Sinister music underscores.*

**COP.** Hello…hello…

 *THE LIGHTS GO OUT!*

A power outage?! Must be the storm. *(Then into the phone.)* Oh, hello Chief? Yes, this is— *(Then.)* Hello? Hello? Are you still there? Is this phone working?

*A dim light now rises on Yvette in the Billiard Room.*

**YVETTE.** *(Alarmed by the darkness.)* E-lo? Oo turned out ze lights?! E-lo?!

*She sees someone in the doorway.*

Oh! It's only you. You scared me! I zought you were ze killer!

*Back to the Cop (a duel scene).*

**COP.** Did somebody cut the line? Hello?

*Back to Yvette…*

**YVETTE.** Oh, did you find a clue? What is zat in your hand?

*A gloved hand holding the Rope emerges from behind Yvette. A noose flies onto her neck! She struggles!*

*Music sting. Lights out.*

*The Billiard Room module retreats in darkness as…*

**COP.** *(Into phone.)* Oh, good you can hear me. You see, I found an abandoned car and wound up in an old mansion, where all the lights just went out. I'm telling you, Chief, there's something funny going on around here.

*A gloved hand holding a Candlestick emerges from a trap door in the bookshelf.*

They're having some sort of a party and you'll never believe who I just saw…

**UNSEEN MURDERER.** Psst.

*The Cop turns around at the sound.*

*The Candlestick descends on the Cop. Music sting.*

**COP.** No!

*Blackout.*

# Scene 13

*The Hall.*

*The pulsating tone of a telephone off the hook is heard. A lighter flickers. In the light of the flame we see Wadsworth's face. He finds the light panel. Suddenly, the lights turn back on revealing Wadsworth fully. The guests pour back onstage.*

**ALL.** *(Relieved at the lights; ad-libbing.)* Ahhh. / Oh, there we are! / Must've been a short in a wire. *(Etc.)*

**PEACOCK.** Let there be light!

**WHITE.** *(Quieting everyone.)* Shhh…

> *Everyone listens.*

Do you hear that?

**GREEN.** Sounds like a telephone is off the hook.

**SCARLET.** It's coming from the Library.

**PEACOCK.** That's where the killer must be!

**WADSWORTH.** *(Smoothing his hair.)* I'm going in!

**SCARLET.** Aren't you afraid?

**WADSWORTH.** Of course.

**PLUM.** Of what? A fate worse than death?

**WADSWORTH.** No…just death.

> *Wadsworth, followed by the guests, goes to the Library door. He unlocks it. The Cop sits, head down.*

*(Timidly, from the doorway.)* Excuse me, Mr. Cop. Are you all right? Do you need assistance? A phone book perhaps?

**PEACOCK.** *(Pushing past Wadsworth.)* Hey! Listen, Copper! The butler asked you a question! Hang up the telephone already, or I will!

> *He doesn't move. She pulls the Cop's body back, revealing a bloody Candlestick protruding from his head morbidly. Music sting!*

> *Peacock screams! The guests scream!*

*Transition music plays as they run out of the Library.*

*The Library module retreats as the Billiard Room module pushes on.*

*The guests hysterically run until they all arrive and settle in the Billiard Room. Their bodies block the view of the billiard table.*

*They all breathe heavily.*

**WADSWORTH.** We should be safe here in the Billiard Room.

*They all inhale/exhale. A moment of peace.*

**WHITE.** I don't feel safe.

**GREEN.** I can't relax.

**PLUM.** How about a round of pool to pass the time?

**ALL.** *(Ad-libbing.)* Oh yes. / I love pool. / Good idea. / Rack 'em up. *(Etc.)*

*They all step aside and reveal Yvette's splayed, strangled body hanging off the table! Music sting!*

*The guests scream! Transition music. The Billiard Room module retreats as the guests run to the Hall, continuing to scream, exiting individually through all remaining doors. The house is quiet.*

*Just then…the doorbell rings. The front door opens on its own. A cute, perky Singing Telegram Girl tap dances in the door frame.*

**YOUNG WOMAN.** *(Singing.)* I…am…YOUR SINGING TELEGRAM…

*Gunshot! The young woman falls dead in the doorway. Slowly and dejectedly, the guests come out of all the doors and notice the sixth dead body in the doorway.*

## Scene 14

*The Conclusion.*

*They collectively take a breath.*

*Wadsworth, pushing the girl's legs out of the way, shuts the front door. They are eerily calm.*

**WADSWORTH.** Three murders in three minutes.

**MUSTARD.** That's our best record.

**GREEN.** Three murders.

**PLUM.** Six altogether.

**WADSWORTH.** This is getting serious.

**SCARLET.** The Cook, Mr. Boddy, the Motorist, the Cop, Yvette, and the Singing Telegram Girl.

**PEACOCK.** But who is the murderer?!

**SCARLET.** Ain't that the million-dollar question.

**WADSWORTH.** Sometimes the most obvious answer is right under our noses. I think the best course of action is to retrace our steps.

> *Wadsworth retraces the entire play, with recreations of benchmark moments and imitations galore, starting at a normal pace and building to a frenzied pace.*

It all started like this…

> *Thunder. Lightning. Music underscores.*

At the start of the evening, there was thunder, lightning, the dogs barked.

*(Imitating the doorbell.)* DING DONG.

*(As Mustard.)* Colonel Mustard.

*(Imitating the doorbell.)* DING DONG.

*(As White.)* Mrs. White.

*(As himself.)* Who noticed Yvette.

> *He replicates the music sting.*

*(As Peacock.)* Mrs. Peacock.

*(As himself.)* Who noticed…

*(As the Cook.)* The Cook.

> *He replicates the music sting.*

*(As himself.)* Then…
*(As Green.)* Mr. Green.

> *He barks.*

*(As himself.)* Sit!

> *He sits—then stands.*

No, not you sir. Please, come in.
*(As Plum.)* Then, Professor Plum.
*(As Scarlet.)* Miss Scarlet.

> *He hits a gong, surprising the guests.*

*(As the Cook.)* Then, dinner is served.
*(As Plum.)* Dinner?! Well, that was more like a cocktail minute.
*(As himself.)* To the Dining Room!

> *He moves. The guests follow.*

*(As Yvette.)* Shark's fin soup.
*(As Peacock, slurping.)* Ooo. My favorite!
*(As himself.)* Then Mr. Boddy arrived and we all went to the Study.

> *He moves in a circle around the guests.*

*(As Yvette.)* Coffee? Brandy?
*(As Scarlet.)* Who is this Mr. Boddy, you brutish butler?
*(As Boddy.)* How d'you do?
*(As himself.)* Then Mr. Boddy asked me to pass out packages.

> *He "passes" out packages swiftly.*

*(As White.)* Ahhh! A snake! No. It's a Rope.
*(As himself.)* Then Mr. Boddy switched off the lights.
*(As Boddy.)* Now!

> *He switches off the lights. Lights go black. They scream!*

> *Lights up. Wadsworth lies dead on the floor. They scream again!*

> *Wadsworth sits up suddenly. They gasp as he continues…*

*(As himself.)* Mr. Boddy was dead. But not really. Really he was alive. But we didn't know it. Then, Mrs. Peacock drank his drink…

> *He drinks from Peacock's flask and spits all over the guests.*

*(As Peacock.)* Poison!

> *He screams. Peacock screams. He screams. He slaps himself.*

*(As Scarlet.)* Well, someone had to stop her screaming!
*(As himself.)* And then we heard…

> *He lip-synchs to a sound cue of Yvette screaming.*

To the Billiard Room! But Mrs. Peacock joined late.
*(As Peacock.)* I'm an old woman who may or may not have been poisoned.
*(As himself.)* Then Mrs. White asked…
*(As White.)* Who else is in the house?
*(As himself.)* To which we all replied…

**ALL.**  *(Looking out.)* ZE COOK!

> *He moves.*

**WADSWORTH.**  Who we found knifed in the back!

> *He mimes stabbing her, then imitates the Cook falling dead*
> *out of the freezer onto Green.*

*(As Green.)* Oh God. Oh God. So gross. Blood. Germs. *(Muffled by his own arm.)* Will somebody help me up!
*(As himself, miming dragging the Cook.)* I suggested we take the Cook's body into the Study.

> *He lies as "dead" Boddy, then hops up, revealing a blank*
> *space!*

*(As himself.)* But Boddy's body was gone!

> *He mimes draping himself over an imaginary Peacock.*

Then Mrs. Peacock entered with Boddy on her body because Boddy had been bludgeoned in his bean. *(Then.)* Then, the briefcase!

> *He mimes opening the briefcase at the desk. They gasp.*

Empty! *(Then.)* Next the Motorist arrived…
*(As Mustard.)* Are you a killer?
*(As himself.)* And I locked *him* in the Lounge!

> *He fake kills Green á la the Motorist, with a mimed Wrench*
> *to the head. Green drops "dead" á la the Motorist.*

Dead!

> *He moves to the front door.*

That's when the unexpected Cop showed up.

(*As Cop.*) Hello…you're all acting rather peculiar.

(*As himself.*) Can you canoe?

> *He fake kills Plum with a mimed Candlestick to the head—Plum drops "dead" á la the Cop.*

Dead! Then the maid got strangled in the Billiard Room!

> *He fake strangles Scarlet with a mimed Rope—Scarlet drops "dead" á la Yvette.*

Dead! Which brings us to…

(*As Singing Telegram Girl.*) I am…

(*Fake shooting.*) BANG!

> *White goes down as if shot.*

> *Everyone is down except Mustard and Peacock.*

(*As himself.*) And here we all are.

**MUSTARD.** (*Clapping.*) Bravo!

> *As they speak, they slowly rise back up.*

**WHITE.** Impressive, Wadsworth.

**PLUM.** But what does it prove?!

**GREEN.** Nothing!

**WADSWORTH.** Well…

**SCARLET.** (*Interrupting.*) Enough of this! I know who the murderer is!

**ALL.** You do?!

**SCARLET.** I do!

**WADSWORTH.** All right then. We're listening, Miss Scarlet. Who do you accuse?

> *Scarlet reveals Plum's pipe, pointing it at Plum.*

**SCARLET.** It was PROFESSOR PLUM, IN THE HALL, WITH THE REVOLVER!

> *They look/gasp.*

**PLUM.** Liar!

**SCARLET.** We all heard the gun go off, Professor! And I found your stupid tobacco pipe here when we were searching the house.

When'd you drop it, huh? While scoping out the best vantage point to kill your next victim?! I bet that poor Singing Telegram Girl was an old patient of yours, right?

**PLUM.** I never saw that girl before in my life! It wasn't me…

**WADSWORTH.** Well. The gun is missing. Gentlemen, turn out your pockets. Ladies, empty your purses. Whoever has the gun, is the murderer.

> *They all do so. Plum pulls out the Revolver with a grunt. He points it at Wadsworth. The guests gasp!*

**GREEN.** Well done, Wadsworth!

**PLUM.** *(Threatening.)* You won't be able to prove anything if you're all dead!

**WADSWORTH.** That may be so, Professor Plum. *(With condescending confidence as he crosses to the front door.)* But if we're alive…

> *He opens the door. The Chief of Police and his backup Cop enter, guns and badge revealed, stepping over the dead Singing Telegram Girl on their way in.*

Officers. *(Pointing at Plum.)* There's your man.

**CHIEF.** Well done, Wadsworth!

**GREEN.** That's what I said!

**CHIEF.** Yes, well, I'm saying it now. I'm Hank Cuffs, Chief of Police. *(Disarming/cuffing Plum.)* And Professor Plum, you're coming with me.

> *Music sting. Cast freezes. Plum breaks the freeze to step forward and say…*

**PLUM.** That's not how it happened! It happened like this…

> *They physically rewind—to the sound of a tape rewinding— back to their starting positions.*

**WADSWORTH.** All right then. We're listening, Professor Plum. Who do you accuse?

> *Plum waves Mustard's medal.*

**PLUM.** It was COLONEL MUSTARD, IN THE LOUNGE, WITH THE WRENCH!

**MUSTARD.** I never lounge!

**PLUM.** I found your medal of honor in the Lounge where the Motorist was killed by a Wrench to the head; and that Wrench belongs to you!

**MUSTARD.** That's a lie!

**WADSWORTH.** The Wrench is missing. Gentlemen, turn out your pockets. Ladies, empty your purses. Whoever has the Wrench, is the murderer.

> *They all do. Mustard pulls out the Wrench with a threatening grunt.*

> *They look/gasp! A bit faster.*

**GREEN.** Well done, Wadsworth!

> *Cops enter. Guns and badge revealed.*

**WADSWORTH.** There's your man, officer. Not a *colonel* of truth in him.

**CHIEF.** Well done, Wadsworth!

**GREEN.** That's what I said!

**CHIEF.** Yes, well, I'm saying it now. Gil T. Verdict. Chief of Police. *(Disarming/cuffing Mustard.)* Colonel Mustard, you're coming with me.

> *Music sting. Cast freezes. Mustard breaks the freeze to step forward and say…*

**MUSTARD.** You have it all wrong! It happened like this…

> *They physically rewind—to the sound of a tape rewinding— a bit faster now…*

**WADSWORTH.** We're listening, Colonel. Who do you accuse?

> *Mustard holds high White's veil.*

**MUSTARD.** It was MRS. WHITE, IN THE BILLIARD ROOM, WITH THE ROPE!

> *They look/gasp!*

**WHITE.** I'd rather die!

**MUSTARD.** I found your veil in the Billiard Room! And I saw how you cringed tonight when Yvette served you dinner.

**WHITE.** Yes, it's true, I knew Yvette…she had a torrid love affair with my late husband. I hated her. I hated her SO MUCH. It…it… the…FLAMES. On the side of my face. Breathing. HEAVING… breaths… But just because I hated her, doesn't mean I killed her!

**WADSWORTH.** The Rope is missing. Gentlemen, turn out your pockets. Ladies…

> *White pulls out the Rope with a yelp. They gasp as she waves it threateningly.*

**GREEN.** Well done, Wadsworth!

> *Cops burst in, faster now.*

**CHIEF.** *(Nearly at the same time.)* Well done, Wadsworth!

**GREEN.** That's what I said!

**CHIEF.** *(Nearly at the same time.)* Yes, well, I'm saying it now. Mark M'Words, Chief of Police. *(Disarming/cuffing White.)* Mrs. White…

> *Music sting. Faster now… Before they even have time to freeze, White shouts…*

**WHITE.** It happened like this…

> *They rewind—to the sound of a tape rewinding—even faster now.*

**WADSWORTH.** Mrs. White, who do you accuse?

> *They barely have time to rewind back to position. White holds Peacock's feather…*

**WHITE.** It was MRS. PEACOCK, IN THE KITCHEN, WITH THE DAGGER! I found your feather by the corpse!

**WADSWORTH.** Gentlemen, turn out your pockets…

> *Peacock reveals a Dagger with a shout.*

**GREEN and CHIEF.** Well done, Wadsworth!

> *Cops enter on Green's line, disarming and cuffing Peacock.*

That's what I said! Yes, well, I'm saying it now.

**CHIEF.** I'm Barry D. Hatchett.

**ALL.** Chief of Police!

**PEACOCK.** But that's not how it happened!

**ALL.** IT HAPPENED LIKE THIS!

*They physically rewind too quickly even for the sound cue…*

**PEACOCK.** It was MISS SCARLET, IN THE LIBRARY, WITH THE CANDLESTICK!

*Before anyone can say anything…*

**CHIEF.** Max E. Mumm. Chief of Police.

**SCARLET.** *(To Wadsworth.)* You can't do this to me!

**WADSWORTH.** Frankly, Miss Scarlet, I don't give a damn.

*Music sting.*

*Then, Wadsworth breaks the freeze and steps forward.*

But—it really happened like this.

*They do one final (irritated/lackluster) rewind.*

I know who the murderer is.

**ALL.** Who?!

**WADSWORTH.** All of you!

*They gasp!*

Freeze!

*Wadsworth reveals a gun.*

Nobody move! You're all killers!

**SCARLET.** You can't prove anything, Mr. Wadsworth!

**WADSWORTH.** I'm not Mr. Wadsworth. I'm Mr. Boddy!

**PEACOCK.** How can you be Mr. Boddy if Boddy bled all over me!

**WADSWORTH.** It wasn't Boddy who was bleeding.

**MUSTARD.** But if Boddy wasn't Boddy…then who was he?

**WADSWORTH.** *(Now with an American accent.) He* was Wadsworth. My butler.

*They gasp.*

**SCARLET.** But if you're the real Mr. Boddy, what was your purpose in dragging this all out?

**WADSWORTH.** Well, when you started murdering people, I decided to roll the dice. See if you'd self-implode. Kill off my entire network of spies and informers. Which you all did, splendidly, by the way. Generously leaving your fingerprints on every glass, doorknob, and…dead body. So, now I have each of you on the hook for murder!

**PEACOCK.** Murder?!

**WADSWORTH.** Bribery for petty crimes is one thing…but murder? Now that could get expensive.

**WHITE.** But why this whole charade?!

**PEACOCK.** The searching of the house, the madness of retracing our steps?!

**WADSWORTH.** It's all part of the game!

**ALL.** Game?!

**WADSWORTH.** Well, yeah, I'm relaxed now, you see. Now that you've killed everyone off—there's no evidence left against me. I've got off…scot-free.

**PLUM.** But the police will be here any minute. You'll never get away with this!

>Wadsworth laughs knowingly.

**MUSTARD.** What's so funny?

**SCARLET.** Nobody's called the police, have they?

**WHITE.** They were never on their way.

**WADSWORTH.** Now, listen up, you reprobates. We're gonna stack the bodies in the cellar, lock the cellar door, leave Boddy Manor one at a time, and forget that any of this ever happened.

**PLUM.** I can't forget all this!

**WADSWORTH.** With murder on the menu, the price of blackmail just tripled!

**PLUM.** Forgotten!

**WADSWORTH.** Now move!

**SCARLET.** Wait a minute! We can all rush him. He's got no more bullets left in that gun.

**WADSWORTH.** Oh, come on, you don't think I'm gonna fall for that old trick.

**SCARLET.** It's not a trick. *(Holding up her fingers.)* There was one shot at Mr. Boddy in the Study, two for the chandelier, two at the Lounge door, and one for the Singing Telegram Girl.

**WADSWORTH.** That's not six.

**SCARLET.** One plus two plus two plus one.

**WADSWORTH.** Uh-uh. There was only one shot that got the chandelier, that's one plus two plus ONE plus one.

**SCARLET.** Even if you were right, that would be one plus one plus two plus one, not one plus two plus one plus one.

**WADSWORTH.** Okay fine. One plus two plus—SHUT UP! Point is, there is one bullet left in this gun, and anybody who moves is gonna get it!

**GREEN.** So, you're just gonna keep blackmailing us and we're all supposed to pretend this never happened?

**WADSWORTH.** *(A childlike mocking of Green's vocalizations.) Soyou'rejustgonnakeepblackmailingusandwe'reallysupposedtoblahbl ahblahblahblah? (Then.)* Of course. Why not?

**GREEN.** I'll tell you why not. *(Drawing a gun.)* Larry Goodman! FBI!

> *They gasp (except Wadsworth).*

The jig is up!

**WADSWORTH.** Or is it?!

> *Wadsworth turns and shoots Green!*

> *Green dodges with* Matrix-*esque finesse.*

**GREEN.** *(Smugly.)* Missed me.

> *Green trains his gun on Wadsworth, who is genuinely now frightened.*

**MUSTARD.** You're FBI?!

**GREEN.** Apparently I'm a dead ringer for Green. He got a letter just like each of you. But he came to the Bureau to ask for help. I took his place tonight so we could have a sting operation.

**PEACOCK.** Some sting! Six people died on your watch!

**GREEN.** I usually work the desk. *(Then.)* My beat is property crime—ya know theft, fraud. That's why I was so tickled when the *real* Mr. Wadsworth risked his neck to drop off a whole briefcase worth of evidence last night.

**PLUM.** You've had the evidence this whole time?!

**GREEN.** It's all here. *(Pulling from a pocket.)* Miss Scarlet's books—including client names and dates of "service," proving she's one of D.C.'s top madams and justifying why she killed the Cop—who's listed here, on her payroll.

**SCARLET.** Gimme that!

> *Scarlet lunges at Green. He staves her off with his gun.*

**GREEN.** *(Pulling from another pocket.)* Ooo, what's this?! A love letter addressed to Professor Plum…

**PLUM.** That's private property!

**GREEN.** That Singing Telegram Girl was the underage daughter of the head of the U-NO WHO, *who* woulda come clean to Daddy—*who* woulda cleaned out Professor Plum. So, you killed her.

**PLUM.** Now see here…

> *Wadsworth makes an attempt to escape—Green trains the gun on him again, grounding him.*

**GREEN.** *(To Wadsworth.)* Uh-uh-uh… *(Now to Mustard—trying to pull the negatives out of his sock.)* And these negatives…

> *He can't pull them out so he tries again.*

And these negati… *(One more time—success.)* And these negatives, Colonel. Quite the regular at Miss Scarlet's "establishment." Bet you couldn't be a Colonel anymore if that Motorist had informed your General where he drives you on Tuesday nights.

**MUSTARD.** I just wanted somebody to talk with!

> *Wadsworth takes a step toward Green's gun. Green thwarts his attempt with Ninja-like moves and carries on with a flourish.*

**GREEN.** Shark's fin soup indeed, Mrs. Peacock. Too bad your old Cook couldn't keep quiet. If only she hadn't blabbed about your briberies, maybe you wouldn't have killed her—just before joining us outside the Billiard Room. Now we know what really took you so long.

**PEACOCK.** Circumstantial evidence will never hold up in a court of law!

**GREEN.** *(Unzipping his pants and pulling it out from his crotch.)* But this notarized record from the Cook will. *(Off of Peacock's disgusted reaction, now to White.)* And Mrs. White…

> *He zips his fly.*

…You weren't lying, were you? You really did hate Yvette.

**WHITE.** *(Reprising her moment.)* Flames…flames on the side—

**GREEN.** OK, we get it. *(Revealing a vial, seemingly out of thin air.)* Here's a container holding fingerprints collected at the scenes of your previous murders—

**WHITE.** I never murdered my husbands!

**GREEN.** Fingerprints I'm sure the FBI will be able to match to those found on the noose tied around Yvette's neck.

**WHITE.** I wore gloves!

**GREEN.** *(Tearing open his vest to reveal White's gloves pinned to his chest.)* You mean these?

> *White turns away á la "Damn."*

And last, but not least, Mr. Bobby Boddy.

**WADSWORTH.** It's Robert.

**GREEN.** Now *you* didn't hate Yvette at all, did you, Mr. Boddy?

**WADSWORTH.** What's it to you?

**GREEN.** "Illicit green-card love affair" is the icing on the cake of this FBI file. An FBI file on the whole Boddy family. Your butler, the *real* Wadsworth, has been feeding us information for months. Talk about a real American.

**WADSWORTH.** He was British.

**GREEN.** You know what I mean. *(Then.)* I see why you'd wanna kill him. Twice. Your shot missed him in the Study. But he wisely played dead. And it wasn't 'til you caught him trying to escape that you bludgeoned him to death with the Lead Pipe I'd dropped on my way to the Kitchen.

**PLUM.** *(To White.)* I mean really, who drops a murder weapon?

**GREEN.** *(Defensive.)* I didn't know it was a murder weapon when I dropped it. *(Back to brass tacks.)* The Boddy family has been wanted for organized crime for generations but they've always eluded the law. Until now.

Tonight, the "Boddy Business" has reached a *dead* end.

**WADSWORTH.** You leave my family out of this!

> *Wadsworth, enraged, uses the Dagger he's snagged from Peacock's purse to lunge at Green…*

> *Green fires, shooting Wadsworth successfully! Everyone gasps!*

Ow! Owwww! You got me, Larry!

> *Falling into Green's arms—here Wadsworth intentionally aims to gross Green out while actively dying—free-form, loose improvisation á la the following:*

I'm getting blood on your nice suit, Larry. Oh, my guts are spilling out all over you. Put pressure on the wound, Larry. Don't be a baby. Really get in there. *(Back on script.)* Put your finger in the hole, Larry! *(Then, springing out of Green's grossed-out arms.)* Second wind!

> *He's back up—maybe with a tap dance and song.*

"If I knew you were coming, I'd have baked you a cake!"

> *Now suddenly down again, clutching his heart, moaning elaborately in pain—then, with a flourish, he appears dead.*

**PLUM.** *(Immediately.)* He's dead!

**WADSWORTH.** *(Immediately back up again.)* Not yet.

**ALL.** Gasp!　　　　　　**PLUM.** *(Disappointed in himself.)* God!

**WADSWORTH.** *(As if the last moment never happened—singing.)* "Smile, when your heart is breaking…smile…" *(Then immediate, searing pain—weak now, he calls to Green—free-form, loose improvisation á la the following.)* Larry. Larry, come closer, Larry. Hold me. It's so cold, Larry. I've got something I need to tell you. One last thing— *(Now back in Green's arms, back on script.)* Always remember…

> *A sudden shift—he smacks Green violently across the face— Green goes reeling, Wadsworth's final burst of strength immediately fades and now, in utter pain, he dies in a cacophony of physicality and vocalizations (to music)—as the rest look on in horror—until one final death rattle and…*

Game over.

*HE DIES FOR REAL.*

**GREEN.**  I tell ya, this was the most exciting night I've had in a long time! *(Then.)* And now, you're all under arrest. *(Toward the front door.)* Officers…

> *Musical fanfare. Cops with guns burst through the front door, posing with Green á la* Charlie's Angels *as the guests hold up their hands.*

Here are the criminals you've been looking for, and you'll find the recordings of the confessions we've been waiting for in the Billiard Room.

**PLUM.**  *(Doh!)* The tapes!

**CHIEF.**  All right. Whodunit?

**ALL.**  *(Each pointing at one of the others.)* He/she did!

**GREEN.**  They all did! But if you want to know who killed Mr. Boddy… *(Indicates Wadsworth.)* It was me. Special Agent Larry Goodman, in the Hall, with my gun.

**CHIEF.**  Well done, Goodman.

**ALL.**  That's what he said!

**GREEN.**  *(Arrogantly twirling his gun.)* And *that's* how it really…

> *His gun goes off! Perhaps the chandelier (or a second chandelier) falls! Everyone screams!*

Sorry. Sorry. *(Back to Chief.)* Okay Chief, take 'em away! I'm going home to sleep with my wife.

> *Bows to music.*

## End of Play

# PROPERTY LIST
*(Use this space to create props lists for your production)*

# SOUND EFFECTS

*(Use this space to create sound effects lists for your production)*